PIC
CANADIAN
ACTORS

The Stories Behind Legends of the Silver Screen

Stone Wallace

FOLK
LORE
PUBLISHING

© 2005 by Folklore Publishing
First printed in 2005 10 9 8 7 6 5 4 3 2 1
Printed in Canada

The Publisher: Folklore Publishing

Website: www.folklorepublishing.com

Library and Archives Canada Cataloguing in Publication

Wallace, Stone, 1957–
Pioneer Canadian actors : the stories behind the legends of the silver screen / Stone Wallace.

(Star biographies)
Includes bibliographical references.
ISBN 1-894864-42-5

1. Actors—Canada—Biography. 2. Actresses—Canada—Biography.
I. Title. II. Series.

PN1998.2.W233 2005   791.4302'8'092271   C2005-902439-9

Project Director: Faye Boer
Project Editor: Nicholle Carrière
Production: Trina Koscielnuk
Cover Design: Valentino & Burch

Cover Images: Courtesy of International Communications Systems

Photography credits: Every effort has been made to accurately credit the sources of photographs. Any errors or omissions should be directed to the publisher for changes in future editions. Photographs courtesy of International Communications Systems.

We acknowledge the support of the Alberta Foundation for the Arts for our publishing program.

PC: P5

Table of Contents

Dedication

Dedicated with affection to my beloved mother-in-law, Paulina Spakowski.

❦

Acknowledgements

WRITING THIS BOOK HAS TRULY BEEN AN ENJOYABLE EXPERIENCE, as most of the actors profiled are legends that I grew up with, either on television series or late shows or watching larger than life on the silver screen. I am sure that many readers will feel the same way.

I would just like to take a moment to thank the people who assisted me in the writing and production of this book. As always, my publisher and friend Faye Boer, who is never too busy to promptly answer my questions regarding the project at hand. I would like to thank my editor Nicholle Carrière, who worked with me on a previous project and did me proud. Once again, she has not let me down. To Dr. Philip Chamberlin, a special acknowledgement both for providing the superb photographic studies of the subjects included, and also for his help in offering personal insight into the lives of veteran stars Mary Pickford and Fay Wray.

My heartfelt appreciation to all of you.

❦

Foreword

A BELATED REALIZATION CAME TO ME EARLY IN 1970 WHILE serving as Curator of Motion Pictures at the Los Angeles County Museum of Art. At the time, I was working on a retrospective tribute to Mary Pickford and learned that an unusually large number of "American" movie stars were born in Canada. Pickford was the most important of these, of course, because she was far and away the most prominent woman in the motion picture field worldwide and a power in the industry equal to, or greater than, any man—including studio heads and producers. By 1920, Pickford had added producer and studio head (United Artists) to her acting credits, thus becoming a triple-threat without peer.

Despite her prominence and the high visibility of other Canadian stars such as Lorne Greene, William Shatner, Fay Wray, Raymond Burr, Donald Sutherland, Glenn Ford and Raymond Massey, few of these are thought of as Canadian. It is almost as if membership in the Hollywood pantheon erases consciousness of birth origin, much as Hollywood erases regional accents in all but the most tenacious of identifying language traits.

Focusing these mini-biographies in a single volume should go a long way towards making movie fans aware of the enormous contribution that Canadians have made to the motion picture field.

–Philip Chamberlin

Introduction

IN MY PREVIOUS BOOK FOR FOLKLORE PUBLISHING, *FAMOUS Canadian Actors*, I explored the lives and careers of many contemporary film players who, though born in this country, went on to achieve their fame and success in Hollywood.

Pioneer Canadian Actors examines the stories behind those actors and actresses who many consider to be our country's pioneers in the motion picture industry. From the movies' first superstar Mary Pickford through the distinguished screen careers of Raymond Massey and Christopher Plummer to the television successes of Lorne Greene, Raymond Burr and William Shatner, these film players have proven themselves strong representatives of Canadian talent. It should also be noted that two of the most powerful Hollywood movie moguls were born in Canada: Louis B. Mayer, president of Metro-Goldwyn-Mayer, and Jack L. Warner, the head of production for Warner Brothers. Silent movie comedy pioneer and Keystone Kops creator Mack Sennett also boasts Canadian roots.

Our country has indeed produced many legendary movie figures who have become part of popular public consciousness. In addition to the names already mentioned, we will also look at the lives of the movies' original horror heroine Fay Wray, the beautiful Norma Shearer, the always-reliable Glenn Ford, the versatile Donald Sutherland, the classical Gordon Pinsent and the zany Leslie Nielsen.

Each of these actors has contributed his or her own unique talent and presence to create film and television roles that have truly become classic and, more importantly, will continue to entertain audiences for years to come.

CHAPTER ONE

Mary Pickford
(1892–1979)

IT IS UNFORTUNATE, BUT MANY PEOPLE TODAY CANNOT begin to imagine the incredible popularity of Mary Pickford during her peak years in motion pictures (1917–29). The reason, however, is not difficult to understand. Many of her great films were made more than 80 years ago, and except for art house showings and occasional runs on television, most people of the current generation don't even recognize the name Mary Pickford.

Admittedly, watching some of her films today, one might wonder what all the fuss was about. Silent films required broad or stylized acting gestures to convey a character's emotions to the audience. While Mary was perhaps one of the more natural performers of the era, on occasion her acting was melodramatic—perhaps respected by an older generation of filmgoers, but mostly jeered at by younger audiences unfamiliar with the art of silent cinema.

Nevertheless, the Canadian-born actress who became known as "America's Sweetheart" was, during the height of her popularity, world famous, and her storybook marriage to the dashing Douglas Fairbanks the most envied love story of its day.

Pickford and Fairbanks were regarded as American royalty, and in their lavish estate, which newspapers dubbed Pickfair, the couple lived majestically, waited on by servants, dining sumptuously and frequently entertaining luminaries from around the world.

The incredible success she would achieve could only have seemed like a fairy tale to the little girl born Gladys Louise Smith on April 8, 1892, in Toronto, Ontario. She was the eldest of three children, big sister to Lottie and baby brother Jack. Although Gladys came from a family with theatrical roots and she started in show business as a child, the family suffered tragedy when Gladys' father, John Charles Smith, died in 1898 at the age of 30, leaving his wife and children nearly penniless. To support her family, Gladys' mother, Charlotte Hennessy Smith, took in boarders and worked a variety of odd jobs, including seamstress. It was while she was preparing costumes for the Cummings Stock Company that the stage manager noticed five-year-old Gladys and cast her in dual roles as both a girl and a little boy in the play *The Silver King*.

Mary was paid eight dollars a week for her work at the Princess Theatre. Encouraged by this "windfall," Charlotte became Gladys' manager and began scouting for more stage work for her daughter. In 1902, they were in New York, where the girl began touring with a series of road companies, billed as "Baby Gladys."

At the age of 14, she landed her first Broadway role in *The Warrens of Virginia*, at which time, at the urging of famed producer David Belasco, she changed her name to Mary Pickford, after her maternal grandfather, John Pickford Hennessey. In 1908, she decided to earn some extra money by doing film work and approached the American Biograph Company for a screen test. She passed her audition and made her movie debut as an extra in *The Lonely Villa*, directed by D.W. Griffith. Griffith asked Mary to return the following day, and Mary agreed—but only if her pay of $5 per day was doubled to $10. After all, she reasoned, she had just starred in a Belasco play.

Mary's next picture, *Mrs. Jones Entertains* (1909), saw her in her first feature role, as Dorothy Nicholson. Soon Mary Pickford was one of the premiere players with Biograph. It is estimated that between 1909 and 1912, Mary had appeared in approximately 150 one-reel pictures. The public was quickly taking notice of the young actress, whom they affectionately referred to as "Little Mary" or "The Girl with Golden Hair." And as Mary's popularity grew, she started exerting more control over her career. She began taking an active hand in the production of her films, with the right to choose both her leading man and director, such as fellow former-Torontonian Allan Dwan, who directed Mary in *The Foundling* (1915).

Her association with Biograph proved fortuitous in another way—it was while doing films for this company that she met her first husband, Owen Moore. Owen began working with Biograph in 1908 and appeared in many of D.W. Griffith's early productions. He was Mary Pickford's stylish leading man in her early films, and they were secretly wed in 1911. Some of their films together include *Cinderella* (1914), in which he played her Prince Charming, and *Mistress Nell* (1915). Mary eventually left Owen for Douglas Fairbanks, whom she met during a World War I war bond tour, and the couple finally divorced in 1920. Owen went on to wed silent film actress Kathleen Perry, a marriage that lasted until his sudden death of a heart attack at age 52.

In 1912, Mary returned to the stage when David Belasco offered her the role of the little blind girl in *A Good Little Devil*. It proved a good move because, after she left Biograph in 1913, Mary signed with Adolph Zukor's Famous Players Film Company (later Paramount Pictures) for the then astronomical sum of $10,000 per week along with an additional $30,000 signing bonus. Zukor had seen Mary in the stage version of *A Good Little Devil* and planned that property as her first feature film. But it was her portrayal of Tessibel Skinner in *Tess of the Storm Country* that really established Mary as a "movie star." She followed that picture with other hits such as *Rebecca of Sunnybrook Farm* (1917) and *The Poor Little Rich Girl* (1917), and she played Sara Crewe in the original version of *The Little Princess*, also in 1917. Her most challenging roles came when she appeared both as the deformed Cockney, Unity Blake, and as the title character in *Stella Maris* (1918). Audiences used to the onscreen innocence of Mary were shocked to see her in the guise of Unity Blake, who, sheltered from life's realities, finds herself hopelessly at odds with humanity and eventually commits murder and suicide.

Yet such was Mary's ongoing popularity, even in this uncharacteristic role, that by the time she was 24 years old, she was earning $350,000 per picture and had become Hollywood's first millionaire.

Part of Mary's enormous wealth came with the formation of the Mary Pickford Corporation, her own production company, an enterprise in which she held a 50/50 partnership with her parent company. In addition, Paramount had established Artcraft, whose sole purpose was to distribute Mary's films and other pictures approved by her.

However, trouble arose when Zukor would not give Mary decisive script approval, and in 1919, she left Paramount and signed an unprecedented deal with First National Pictures for $675,000 per film against 50 percent of the gross! In addition, she was allowed complete control over her productions.

But after only one year and three pictures for the studio (*Daddy-Long-Legs*, *The Heart o' the Hills* and *The Hoodlum*), Mary decided to become her own boss and together with second husband Douglas Fairbanks, whom she had wed in March 1920, Charlie Chaplin and her old Biograph director D.W. Griffith, she formed the United Artists Corporation. This afforded the players not only the potential for increased profits, but also gave them their own studio and distribution network. It was through United Artists that all of Mary's subsequent films were released.

Much of Mary's popularity with audiences came from her convincing portrayals of characters much younger than herself. This was tested to the extreme in 1920, when 27-year-old Mary essayed the role of 12-year-old Pollyanna. Fortunately, she pulled it off, and *Pollyanna* was a major success.

The next year, she appeared in *Little Lord Fauntleroy*, taking on the roles of both the title character and the mother. This would be the last film in which she would play a dual role, even though she was convincing in both parts.

But after reprising the role of Tessibel Skinner in the remake of *Tess of the Storm Country* (1922), Mary decided she wanted to "grow up," and she cut her long trademark curls into a short bob in order to present a more mature look.

In an attempt to further change her image, she imported German director Ernst Lubitsch to America to film *Rosita* (1923). Despite rumours of on-set dissention between Mary and Lubitsch, the movie did establish Mary Pickford as an actress of substance, with critics applauding her performance as the feisty street singer who rises to prominence in

the court of a philandering king, played by actor
Holbrook Blinn.

Mary appeared in another adult role in the Eliza-
bethan drama *Dorothy Vernon at Haddon Hall* (1924),
which she also directed, though she did not receive
a director's credit. The film did poorly at the box
office—a rarity in Mary's career—testimony that
audiences preferred to see her in her more recognizable roles. Perhaps with more than a little reluc-
tance, Mary returned to the role of a child for her
next two films. In the tenement drama *Little Annie
Rooney* (1925), Mary is the 12-year-old title character (she was 32 at the time) who sets out with
her brother Tim (Gordon Griffith) to avenge the
murder of their policeman father (Walter James)
committed by the boy she loves (William Haines).
The movie wasn't one of Mary's stronger vehicles,
but the next year she starred in the classic film
Sparrows. Again cast as a youth, her character, the
orphan Molly, proves herself extremely resourceful
in her attempt to protect her fellow orphans from
their evil captor Mr. Grimes, played to malevolent
perfection by Gustav von Seyffertitz.

Sparrows remains one of the best-remembered
films of the silent era, with its atmospheric sets,
dark, sinister plot and suspenseful climax that takes
place in an alligator-infested swamp. Although
again older than her character, 33-year-old Mary
delivered an effective, believable performance as
Molly.

As evidence of Mary's popularity at the time, while she and Douglas Fairbanks were on an around-the-world tour, the couple found themselves greeted at the Moscow train station by a crowd of 300,000 people. The incident wasn't unique, as they received similar receptions in London, Paris, Rome, Berlin, Stockholm and Tokyo.

Either as a gimmick or perhaps because she genuinely wanted to participate in the material, at the height of her career Mary chose to play two uncredited "bits." In the blockbuster *Ben-Hur* (1925), she is a crowd extra in the chariot race scene. Then in *The Black Pirate* (1926), starring her husband, Douglas Fairbanks, she is the double for leading lady Billie Dove in the final embrace.

Mary next appeared as Maggie Johnson opposite future husband, band leader and actor Charles "Buddy" Rogers in the sweet romantic comedy *My Best Girl* (1927), and then she turned up again *sans* billing as the Virgin Mary in then hubby Fairbanks' *The Gaucho*.

One of Mary's lasting achievements was her role in founding the Academy of Motion Picture Arts and Sciences (AMPAS) in 1926. By the mid-1920s, the movie industry had grown from its early days as a nickelodeon novelty to the fourth largest industry in America. While in Moscow, Mary and Douglas Fairbanks had been impressed by the Soviet Film Institute and, on their return, proposed to MGM head Louis B. Mayer the idea of an American film academy. Mary Pickford spearheaded the proposal, but Fairbanks and Mayer were also involved. All told, 36 industry people helped to form AMPAS.

Mary experienced personal sorrow when her mother Charlotte passed away in March 1928. Mary was devastated and reacted almost violently to her mother's death. The two had maintained an extremely close personal and professional relationship, with Charlotte taking an active hand in Mary's contract negotiations and her other business affairs.

Despite her loss, Mary continued to work, and in 1929, she received an Oscar for her role as Norma Besant in *Coquette*. This proved a double coup for Mary as the film was also her first talking part, and the Academy recognition was acknowledgement that she had successfully survived the transition to sound.

Sadly, her movie career peaked with *Coquette*. In the film adaptation of William Shakespeare's *The Taming of the Shrew* (1929), Mary finally had the opportunity to work with husband Douglas Fairbanks for the first and only time. However, it was not a pleasant shoot, as Mary and Fairbanks' marriage was starting to deteriorate. The major reason for the strain was Fairbanks' indiscreet infidelities. Bad luck further plagued the picture—while the film was received favourably by critics, with the *New York Times* proclaiming it as "one of the 10 best pictures of the year," its October 29 release date coincided with the collapse of the stock market.

While the movie was not a flop, it was nowhere near the hit it was expected to be. It later gained notoriety among film buffs for its source credit: "By William Shakespeare, with additional dialogue by Sam Taylor."

Mary made just three more talkies—*Forever Yours* (1930), *Kiki* (1931) and *Secrets* (1933)—before permanently retiring from the screen at the age of 41. Although no longer active as a movie actress, Mary kept busy on the board of United Artists and produced movies such as *One Rainy Afternoon* (1936) and the suspense thriller *Sleep, My Love* (1948). Although she was uncredited, she also produced the last movie featuring the Marx Brothers as a team, *Love Happy* (1949), which also had in its cast British Columbia–born Raymond Burr as the principal heavy. In 1934, she began working on radio, headlining a cast of actors in various radio dramatizations. She offered that she considered radio to be "the greatest entertainment medium in the world." In 1935, she even tried her hand at writing, publishing a novel titled *The Demi-Widow*.

However, despite these professional satisfactions, the next few years were personally difficult ones for Mary. In 1935, she and Fairbanks finally divorced. Her younger brother Jack had passed away in 1933, followed by sister Lottie, who succumbed to a heart attack in 1936. Ex-husband Douglas Fairbanks died suddenly of a heart attack on December 12, 1939. The great screen athlete was only 56.

On June 24, 1937, Mary wed her former co-star Charles "Buddy" Rogers. Even though Rogers was 12 years her junior, the marriage lasted 42 years until Mary's death. The couple even adopted two children, Ronald and Roxanne, in 1943.

Mary still retained her business savvy. Following her divorce from Fairbanks, Mary and Charlie Chaplin bought out their partners at United Artists, gaining sole control. When Mary finally sold her shares in February 1956, she realized a $3-million profit (Chaplin had sold his remaining shares the year before for $1.1 million). She also owned the copyrights to many of her early films and virtually all of her United Artists output. Initially, she had planned to have the films destroyed following her death, believing they offered little in the way of artistic value, but she later decided to donate the prints to the American Film Institute for preservation.

Throughout her retirement, Mary continued to receive film offers. The one proposal that most interested her was the role of faded movie queen Norma Desmond in director Billy Wilder's *Sunset Boulevard* (1950). But Mary turned down the part after disagreeing with Wilder on several story points.

Mary published her autobiography, *Sunshine and Shadows*, in 1956. At the same time, she began spending more time on her charitable endeavours, such as establishing the Motion Picture County Home and Hospital, whose purpose was to aid industry people unable to pay for retirement lodgings or, if ailing, hospitalization.

However, in later years, ill health and a propensity for alcohol made Mary increasingly reclusive, and she virtually isolated herself in her bedroom at Pickfair. When she was awarded an honorary Oscar at the 1976 Academy Awards, she was unable to attend the ceremony and had her acceptance pre-taped from her estate.

Mary Pickford, who at the peak of her popularity, was known not only as "America's Sweetheart," but "The World's Sweetheart," died of a cerebral hemorrhage on May 28, 1979, at the age of 87.

Throughout her acting career, Mary accumulated a number of "firsts." She was the first star ever to receive a cinematic close-up shot, in the 1912 movie *Friends*. She was also the first star, along with her husband Douglas Fairbanks, to officially place her hand and footprints into the cement outside Grauman's Chinese Theatre, an act that has now become almost a ritual for film stars of distinction.

Mary was proud of her Canadian heritage, but had lost her citizenship when she married her first husband, Owen Moore. In later years, she said: "I wanted to be a Canadian again because of my mother and father," and sought to regain her citizenship status. Six months before she died, Canada's Secretary of State John Roberts formally notified her that she was once again recognized as a citizen of Canada.

CHAPTER TWO

~⊙℃~

Raymond Massey
(1896–1983)

RAYMOND MASSEY NEVER ACHIEVED THE RECOGNITION deserving a man of his vast talent and ability. He was a versatile actor who could play the hero or villain with equal conviction and was at home performing his craft in all mediums. He was an accomplished and much lauded stage and film performer, but he never thumbed his nose at television as did many of his contemporaries. In fact, he probably received his greatest public acknowledgement for his portrayal of the gruff yet kindly Dr. Gillespie on the popular *Dr. Kildare* television series (1961–66). But singling him out for that one role would hardly do Raymond Massey justice. His long and impressive career speaks for itself.

Raymond Hart Massey was born in Toronto, Ontario, on August 30, 1896. It was never intended that he pursue a career in show business, as he and older brother Vincent were the sons of one of the wealthiest families in Canada, their ancestors having immigrated to Canada in 1629. The Massey family made its fortune by manufacturing farm equipment. In 1891, the Massey firm

merged with the Harris Company to form Massey-Harris. A later merger with the Ferguson Company produced Massey-Harris-Ferguson, later shortened to Massey-Ferguson in 1957. Vincent would later become famous in his own right and enjoy an illustrious political career, eventually becoming the first native-born Governor General of Canada, a post he held from 1952 to 1959.

Raymond and Vincent enjoyed a comfortable, privileged childhood. Raymond first discovered an interest in acting while attending Appleby College in Oakville. Later, he appeared in stage productions while enrolled at the University of Toronto and then at Balliol College in Oxford, England.

However, his desire to pursue a theatrical career was put on hold by the outbreak of World War I. Raymond enlisted in the Canadian Field Artillery and was stationed in Siberia during its occupation by American forces. To relieve the boredom of this posting, he began organizing and appearing in shows to entertain the troops who were on occupation duty. Towards the end of the war, Raymond was shipped to France, where he was twice wounded in combat, once seriously.

Discharged from the army because of his injury, Raymond returned home to Canada. While still harbouring a desire to seek a career on the stage, Raymond knew he was expected to join the family's farm implement business. His brother Vincent also came to work for the company after the war.

Vincent was more content to adapt to the business world than his restless brother, and by the early 1920s, Vincent had become the president of Massey-Harris.

Raymond, on the other hand, made the decision to follow his passion and finally convinced his parents to let him go to England to study acting. His father, a staunch Methodist, had relented only on the condition that Raymond agree not to perform in rehearsals on Sunday. Raymond consented, but it was a promise he would not keep.

At first he had a difficult time because the English thought him "too American." However, he worked at his craft, and in 1922, he made his professional debut at the Everyman Theatre, appearing in the play *In the Zone*. Raymond quickly established himself as a stage actor of power and presence, and he appeared in many other plays throughout the 1920s. In addition, he achieved a respected reputation as both a producer and director, directing about 30 plays in London.

As his professional life evolved, so too did his family life, and in 1921 he married Margery Fremantle. Their union produced a son, Geoffrey, who would go on to become an architect. The marriage did not last, however, and the couple divorced in 1929.

As his popularity grew, Raymond began receiving offers from motion picture companies. In 1928, he appeared in his first film, the futuristic (set in

1950) *High Treason*, in which he played the minor role of a pacifist. After completing the film, he was eager to return to live theatre.

In 1931, he appeared on Broadway as the title character in *Hamlet*. Following his success in that role, he received an offer to return to England to play Sherlock Holmes in the film *The Speckled Band*, based on the writings of Sir Arthur Conan Doyle. Raymond gave a creditable performance as the clever sleuth, but most critics found the movie slow moving and dull. However, the film did introduce Raymond Massey to moviegoers, and the following year, he travelled to the United States to appear as Philip Waverton, one of a group of travellers forced to spend the night in James Whale's *The Old Dark House*. This genre classic co-starred Boris Karloff, Charles Laughton and a very young Gloria Stuart of *Titanic* fame.

His second marriage, following rapidly on the heels of his divorce in 1929, was to Adrianne Allen, a union that lasted through 1939. Together they had two children: a daughter, Anne, and a son, Daniel, both of whom would go on to distinguished acting careers. Despite the demands of his young family, Raymond worked on both sides of the Atlantic, alternating between the stage and film. His next movie role was as Citizen Chauvelin in *The Scarlet Pimpernel* (1934), where he was given the opportunity to chew the scenery with his sadistic villainy.

Things to Come (1936) is probably the best known of Raymond's early films. In the movie, based on the futuristic novel by H.G. Wells, Raymond plays John Cabal, the leader of the new world. Although technically dated today, at the time of its release, the film was critically lauded for its visually stunning depiction of the future.

The year 1937 was an extremely prolific one for Raymond Massey—he appeared in five films. In *Fire Over England,* he played the villainous King Philip II of Spain, co-starring with Laurence Olivier in this historical drama detailing the British-Spanish conflict of the 1500s. He was afforded a more sympathetic part as a lonely violinist loved by the married Elisabeth Bergner in *Dreaming Lips.* But then it was back to villainy in his next three films—he played Cardinal Richelieu in *Under the Red Robe,* the scheming "Black Michael" in *The Prisoner of Zenda* and the vindictive Governor Eugene De Laage in John Ford's *The Hurricane.*

The following year saw Raymond's evil Prince Ghul thwarted by Sabu and his band in the colourful action adventure *Drums.* Perhaps Raymond was such a popular villain because he refused to play one-dimensional characters. Instead, he added a personal intelligence to his portrayals, shading his sinister characterizations with a scheming sophistication not generally found in movie villainy.

However, if Raymond feared typecasting, he needn't have worried. After playing an innocent man accused of murder in *Black Limelight*, he returned to America, where he performed his most benevolent and best-loved role to date, that of Abraham Lincoln in *Abe Lincoln in Illinois* (1940). Raymond had first played the role on Broadway in 1938 in Robert Sherwood's Pulitzer Prize–winning play. He was so successful in the part that there was little question he would be asked to reprise the role on film.

While Raymond's gaunt, piercing appearance served him well in his parade of villains, it likewise gave the actor a striking resemblance to the 16th U.S. president. Another interesting side note is that during an early Raymond Massey stage appearance, Robert Todd Lincoln, the late president's son, was in the audience and later remarked how similar Raymond's speaking voice was to his father's.

Abe Lincoln in Illinois was a major critical and financial success and an inspiration to a country soon to be at war. Critics were unanimous in their praise of Raymond's uncanny impersonation of the Great Emancipator, and the actor was nominated for an Academy Award for his masterful work.

As a result of his success, Raymond was signed by Warner Brothers to play another historical character of the period, albeit one far removed from the quiet sincerity of Abraham Lincoln. In *Santa Fe Trail*, Raymond played the fiery, fanatical abolitionist John Brown. While the film itself was far from historically accurate and the lead casting absurd (Errol Flynn as Jeb Stuart and Ronald Reagan as George Custer), Raymond gave a most effective performance as an obsessed man willing both to kill and die for his convictions.

He returned to England for his next film, the suspenseful *49th Parallel* (1941). Raymond was part of a strong British cast that included Leslie Howard and Laurence Olivier in this story about the survivors of a sunken German U-boat trying to avoid capture by making their way from northern Canada into the still-neutral United States. Raymond played the somewhat uncharacteristic role of Andy Brock, a wisecracking AWOL Canadian soldier. All three lead actors worked for half their normal salaries to support the war effort.

After participating in a picture of which he could justifiably feel proud, Raymond found himself back at Warner playing Dr. Ingersoll, a Nazi spy chasing after amnesiac secret agent Nancy Coleman in the rather routine *Dangerously They Live* (1942), starring John Garfield. The film was as unimaginative as its tagline: "Suspense that makes every whisper on the street echo like thunder!"

Raymond was cast as a somewhat more colourful villain, King Cutler, in the big-budget Cecil B. DeMille adventure *Reap the Wild Wind* (1943). But even with a cast that included John Wayne, Ray Milland, Paulette Goddard and Susan Hayward, the film's real star was its Oscar-winning special effects, highlighted by a "to-the-death" undersea battle between Wayne and Milland and a giant octopus.

Raymond was reunited with *Santa Fe Trail* co-stars Errol Flynn and Ronald Reagan in *Desperate Journey*. He played Major Otto Baumeister, a Nazi on the trail of downed American airmen trying to cross the border out of Germany. More World War II propaganda followed in *Action in the North Atlantic* (1943). Raymond played Captain Steve Jarvis in this exciting salute to the merchant marines. His co-star on the film was Humphrey Bogart, who was to become one of Raymond's closest friends.

One afternoon during the making of the picture, Raymond and Humphrey were enjoying a liquid lunch that ended in a wager between the two of who was the braver. Stuntmen had been hired to double for the stars in a difficult shot in which they were to jump off a burning ship into a large, water-filled tank that substituted for the ocean, parts of which had been set ablaze with gasoline. The two by-now-tipsy actors insisted on doing the shot themselves, each thinking that the other would back out at the last minute. But neither did, and both performed the stunt. Both also received minor burns, but their friendship was solidified.

One of Raymond's most offbeat roles of the 1940s was as the murderous Jonathan Brewster in Frank Capra's hilarious *Arsenic and Old Lace* (1944). He played the part that his *Old Dark House* co-star Boris Karloff had made famous on Broadway. In the film, Raymond somewhat resembled Boris, allowing for the famous stage line "I killed him because he said I look like Boris Karloff" to be retained for the movie.

Enjoying his Hollywood success and tired of travelling between two homes in England and the U.S., Raymond decided in 1941 to settle permanently in America with his third wife, Dorothy Whitney, whom he had married in 1939. He became a U.S. citizen in 1944, explaining that both his mother and paternal grandmother had been Americans. Commenting on his roles in films on both sides of the Atlantic, Raymond once said: "I'm Canadian by birth, but the Americans think I'm British, and the British think I'm an American."

Raymond's next important film was the thriller *The Woman in the Window* (1945), directed by Fritz Lang. Raymond played District Attorney Frank Lalor, who begins to unravel the "perfect murder" committed by his friend Edward G. Robinson.

Raymond went back to war for his last two films of the year, though playing on opposite sides. In *God is My Co-Pilot*, based on the memoirs of WWII fighter pilot Robert L. Scott, he played the stern but understanding air force commander Major General Claire L. Chennault, who permits Scott the opportunity to fly with the famed Flying Tigers. In *Hotel Berlin*, he reverted to a role he'd already played to perfection—that of an unsympathetic Nazi, in this case, Arnim von Dahnwitz.

Raymond returned to England in 1946 to appear in Michael Powell's beautifully crafted *Stairway to Heaven*, the story of an RAF pilot (David Niven) killed during WWII who believes his death was unjust and must plead his case before a Heavenly court. Raymond was billed down the cast list as Abraham Farlan.

Raymond enjoyed two further memorable roles as the 1940s drew to a close. Perhaps drawing upon his own military experiences as a soldier with the Canadian army during World War II, he brought the necessary authority to his role as Brigadier General Ezra Mannon in *Mourning Becomes Electra* (1947). Then in 1949, he appeared as Gail Wynard in *The Fountainhead*, Ayn Rand's story about one man's idealism, which starred Gary Cooper.

Unfortunately, with perhaps one or two exceptions, the 1950s saw the talented actor appearing in more conventional film roles. He began the decade by co-starring with buddy Humphrey Bogart in *Chain Lightning* (1950), but Bogie's career had gone into a temporary decline after he left Warner Brothers, and the movie was quickly forgotten.

So was *Come Fill the Cup* (1951), in which Raymond co-starred with James Cagney, who played a recovering alcoholic. The film had promise as a serious study into alcoholism, *à la The Lost Weekend* (1945), but the studio's insistence on adding a melodramatic subplot involving gangsters turned the movie into an incoherent hodgepodge.

A film that offered a bit of irony for the actor was *Prince of Players* (1955), in which Raymond played Junius Brutus Booth, the father of Lincoln's assassin, John Wilkes Booth (John Derek). This, of course, was based on Raymond's celebrated portrayals of Abraham Lincoln. In his career, Raymond had the distinction of playing Lincoln on four separate occasions, thus making the character truly his own.

In 1955, he also reprised his second most famous character, the abolitionist revolutionary John Brown, in *Seven Angry Men*, though, unlike *Santa Fe Trail*, the focus of the picture was entirely on the character and his family.

Perhaps Raymond's best role of the decade was in *East of Eden* (1955) playing the father of a troubled James Dean. Based on the book by John Steinbeck and directed by Elia Kazan, the film was a tremendous box office success, though, of course, most of the accolades went to the dynamic Dean in his first important film role.

Fortunately, Raymond fared better on the stage, even writing a play, *The Hanging Judge*, which was presented on Broadway in 1952. His other important stage endeavours included *John Brown's Body* (1952), *Julius Caesar* (1955) and *The Tempest* (1955). His final Broadway performance was in 1958, when he played God in *J.B.*

With the size and quality of his film parts decreasing, Raymond expanded his talents into the burgeoning medium of television. He appeared in many of the popular programs of the day such as *Climax!*, *Robert Montgomery Presents*, *Playhouse 90* and *Alfred Hitchcock Presents*. Each afforded him a mini-drama that still challenged his dramatic ability but did not compromise his artistic integrity. The fact that Raymond enjoyed keeping busy at his craft is perhaps best exemplified by his guest appearances on such less-demanding television fare as *The Girl from U.N.C.L.E.* and *I Spy*.

He certainly fared better as Dr. Leonard Gillespie on *Dr. Kildare*, a role he played for five years, opposite Richard Chamberlain's idealistic young title character. Ironically, while Raymond had no compunction about appearing on television, he never watched himself on TV, always considering himself a stage and film actor.

But it was perhaps all a comedown for the distinguished thespian who had become relegated to unimportant supporting roles. Except for another portrayal as Abraham Lincoln in John Ford's epic *How the West was Won* (1962), his final film appearances were disappointing. They culminated in a brief part, The Preacher, in his last motion picture, *MacKenna's Gold* (1969), a film in which he shared screen time with other stars of yesteryear such as Edward G. Robinson, Burgess Meredith and Lee J. Cobb.

An aged Raymond last performed in three made-for-television movies. He had the opportunity to once more exert his authoritative presence when he played Secretary of State Freeman Sharkey in *The President's Plane is Missing* (1973). But in between, he took on the less-demanding role of the grandfather, Matthew Cunningham, in *All My Darling Daughters* (1972) and its sequel, *My Darling Daughters' Anniversary*. Charming stuff, to be sure, but hardly an appropriate close to a career as distinguished as Raymond Massey's.

Still, Raymond in his later years had much of which to be proud. His stage, film and television accomplishments had inspired two of his children, Daniel and Anne (from his second marriage), to pursue acting careers. He could also take pride in his family heritage. Besides his brother Vincent's political achievements, he had as a significant historical reference point Toronto's Massey Hall, which had been purchased by his grandfather in 1894 for $150,000.

But of course, Raymond had his own story to tell. He wrote two acclaimed autobiographies: *When I Was Young* and *A Thousand Lives*.

Unlike many great stars of his generation, Raymond remained revered in his later years, though crippling ill health rendered him virtually immobile. His last broadcast appearance was a CBC interview for a program appropriately titled *Actor of the Century*.

Raymond Massey was predeceased by his wife Dorothy, who passed away in July 1982. Raymond died of pneumonia on July 29, 1983.

The film community he had served so well honoured Raymond Massey with two plaques along Hollywood's Walk of Fame. For his contribution to the art of cinema, he received a star at 1719 Vine Street. For his vast body of television work, a second star was placed at 6708 Hollywood Boulevard.

At his funeral, Raymond was eulogized as being not only a fine actor, but also "a scholar and a gentleman."

Given Raymond Massey's impressive list of accomplishments, he could not have been accorded a more accurate and fitting tribute.

CHAPTER THREE

Lorne Greene
(1915–1987)

LORNE GREENE COULD BEST BE DESCRIBED NOT ONLY AS THE patriarch of the famed *Bonanza* Cartwright clan, but also a father figure to a generation of Canadian actors who respected and revered him and benefited from both his wisdom and generosity.

Lorne enjoyed a long and distinguished career as a CBC broadcaster, celebrated stage performer and motion picture actor. But no one can deny that he achieved his greatest and most lasting success as Ben Cartwright, the stern-but-fair father of Adam, Hoss and Little Joe. In fact, Lorne was voted number two by *TV Guide* in its list of the "50 Greatest TV Dads of All Time." It's easy to understand why *Bonanza* enjoyed a 14-year television run (1959–73). Lorne received countless letters from fans (mostly from young boys) wishing that they had him as their father. Ben Cartwright's main quality was that he never shirked his parental duty. His sons knew that whatever the circumstances, they could always depend on him for guidance and support.

Lorne understood that it was a role with responsibilities, but it wasn't difficult for him to play.

He often said that he merely patterned the part after his own father, Daniel, whom Lorne recalled as a man who "didn't have to punish; all he had to do was look." Lorne thought that he could never be like his father in real life, but that he could portray those qualities as an actor.

Lorne Hyman Greene was born on February 12, 1915, in Ottawa, Canada. His parents, Daniel and Dora Greene, were Russian-Jewish immigrants who had already lost their first child, a son, who had died in infancy. Raised as an only child, Lorne idolized his father, who had opened a shop that manufactured orthopedic shoes and boots. But Lorne was not inclined to follow in his father's footsteps. He discovered a love of theatre while attending Lisgar Collegiate Institute. Although at first he was more interested in playing basketball, his already powerful voice got him cast him in the play *Les Deux Sourds*, as one of the deaf characters who must shout throughout the play.

Lorne attended Queen's University in Kingston, Ontario. He enrolled as a chemical engineering student to please his father but could not deny his passion for the theatre. He switched his major to languages so that he could have more time to participate in school plays, and he became active in the university's drama guild—not only as an actor, but also as a director and producer. Upon his 1937 graduation from Queen's with a bachelor of arts degree, Lorne was rewarded with a fellowship to the Neighborhood Playhouse in New York, where he studied with Stanford Meisner and even attended the Martha Graham School of Contemporary Dance. Even after he had become a successful actor, Lorne retained close ties to his alma mater, and in 1971, he was awarded an honorary doctorate.

Following his studies in the U.S., Lorne returned to Canada in 1939. He had married Rita Hands in 1938—a union that in 1945 produced two children, twins Charles and Belinda Susan. Although Lorne was frustrated in his attempts to find stage work, there were opportunities in radio, and Lorne, with his rich baritone voice, was immediately hired as an announcer of the nightly news with the Canadian Broadcasting Corporation. His commanding voice quickly advanced him in his profession and soon, besides his announcing chores, he was also providing the narration for films and documentaries.

Where Lorne really found his niche was as the "Voice of Doom," reporting to an anxious nation developments on the war front during World War II. Soon that ominous title was changed to the "Voice of Canada." A Canadian columnist went so far as to describe Lorne's voice as "surely one of the finest ever wrought by nature." Soon that voice was even heard performing in radio dramas. In 1942, NBC awarded Lorne Greene their top announcing award, a deserved but unique honour in that Lorne was the only Canadian ever to be so acknowledged.

Lorne served with the Royal Canadian Air Force during World War II. Upon his discharge, he returned to his radio duties with the CBC. However, a contract dispute over the freelance voice-over work that Lorne had done resulted in his leaving the network (and a $70,000 yearly salary) and becoming the co-founder of the Jupiter Theatre in Toronto, where he directed and acted in over 50 plays.

In 1946, Lorne founded the Academy of Radio Arts in Toronto. The school prospered, graduating over 400 students, many of whom affectionately referred to Lorne as "Dean Greene."

An inventor as well as a performer, Lorne travelled to New York in 1950 to promote a stopwatch he had created that ran backwards, developed to aid radio announcers in determining the airtime available during broadcasts. Although he was not able to solicit interest in his invention, he ran into former teacher Fletcher Markle from the radio academy, who was a producer on the early television show *Studio One*. He offered Lorne the role of Big Brother in a live broadcast of George Orwell's *1984*. Lorne eagerly accepted and performed so well in the part that he was soon in demand for other lucrative television roles.

Embracing his new success, he decided to close his radio school and stay in New York, where in

1953, he appeared on Broadway opposite Katherine Cornell in *The Prescott Proposal*. Lorne's talents were also quickly recognized by Hollywood, and he was cast in a series of motion pictures throughout the 1950s. He made his screen debut as the Apostle Peter in *The Silver Chalice* (1954), which also introduced Paul Newman to the screen. Unhappily, the film was later voted as one of the 50 worst of all time. Even Paul Newman professed embarrassment at having appeared in it and would later take out a famous Hollywood trade ad apologizing for the film.

Lorne's next appearance was as gangster Benjamin Costain opposite Edward G. Robinson and Ginger Rogers in the suspenseful crime thriller *Tight Spot* (1955). He continued to work alongside an impressive array of co-stars, including Joan Crawford in *Autumn Leaves* (1956), Lana Turner in *Peyton Place* (1957) and Charlton Heston and Yul Brynner in the Anthony Quinn–directed *The Buccaneer* (1958). In between film and television roles, he also performed at the Stratford Festival.

In a 1959 episode of the popular western series *Wagon Train* titled "The Vivian Carter Story," Lorne played (ironically) a widower with three children. Producer David Dortort was in the process of casting for his own western series to be called *Bonanza,* and once he saw Lorne in the *Wagon Train* role, he knew he had found his Ben Cartwright.

Lorne was determined to become a star, but he knew that with the changes in the motion picture industry owing to the popularity of television, his chances were slim of making it in the movies. So far he'd played only supporting roles in his seven films. On *Bonanza* he would be part of an ensemble that included Pernell Roberts as the cool Adam, Dan Blocker as the comical Hoss and a youthful Michael Landon as the hot-tempered heartthrob Little Joe. But Lorne's would be the dominant character.

The series was not an immediate success. In its first year, *Bonanza* suffered in the ratings against the popular *Perry Mason*, which starred fellow Canadian Raymond Burr.

Lorne personally had two problems with the show. First, he objected to the character of Ben Cartwright, who in the first season was presented as a cold, basically unsympathetic character, distant even to his own sons. He felt there was nothing to attract audience interest either to him or the show. He discussed his objection with producer Dortort, who agreed to Lorne's suggestion to fashion Ben more into a version of Lorne's own father.

Lorne's second problem was not quite as easy to solve. He'd never learned to ride a horse, and even after taking lessons, he never became completely comfortable atop one.

In 1960, Lorne finally divorced wife Rita, from whom he had separated in 1953. In 1961, at 46, Lorne married 28-year-old Nancy Ann Deale, who had appeared in an episode of *Bonanza* the previous year. Interestingly, Nancy had been a student at Lorne's Academy of Radio Arts. In 1968, Lorne became a father for the third time when Nancy gave birth to baby Gillian.

By 1964, Lorne was at the peak of his career. *Bonanza* was the top-rated show on television, and he was enjoying personal success with his recording career. On October 31, his western ballad *Ringo* reached number one in *Billboard Magazine*, remaining on the charts for 12 weeks.

But in 1973, after 14 successful seasons, *Bonanza* was cancelled by NBC owing to poor ratings and the death of Dan Blocker the previous year.

Although Lorne was a wealthy man thanks to the show and shrewd investments, he gave no thought to retiring. Instead, he returned to television, starring as Wade Griffin on the short-lived detective series *Griff* (1973–74). He next appeared as Commander Adama in the likewise prematurely terminated science-fiction adventure *Battlestar Galactica* (1978–79) and played another Ben Cartwright–like patriarch, Chief Joe Rorchek, on *Code Red* (1981). His most successful post-*Bonanza* series was *Lorne Greene's New Wilderness* (1982–86), which he hosted and also produced with his son. Lorne maintained a lifelong dedication to conservation and at one time was chairman of the National Wildlife Foundation.

Following his run with *Bonanza*, Lorne returned to film work after a 10-year absence. Perhaps his most important roles were in the all-star disaster epic *Earthquake* (1974) and the top-rated miniseries *Roots* (1977). He truly reached the nadir of his career with his insert footage in the Japanese-produced *Tidal Wave* (1975)—though he was appropriately cast as a newscaster—intended to attract North American audiences.

Lorne Greene finally received his star on Hollywood's Walk of Fame on February 15, 1985. Sadly, though, his health had begun to fail. He suffered hearing loss, which he suspected was caused by all the gunfights he had participated in on *Bonanza*. Apparently, Lorne was a vain man. He refused to wear a hearing aid, just as he was not willing to be seen without his hairpiece. Michael Landon was fond of telling the story of a time when Lorne was submerged in water during an episode of *Bonanza*, lost his toupée and almost drowned because he refused to allow the cast and crew to see him without hair.

Lorne made his final appearance as General Sam Houston in the TV movie *The Alamo: Thirteen Days to Glory*. He had just signed a contract with David Dortort to once more reprise the role of Ben Cartwright in a new TV film, *Bonanza: The Next Generation*, when he entered the hospital for surgery on a perforated ulcer. Complications set in, and Lorne Greene passed away of pneumonia on September 11, 1987, at the age of 72.

The *Bonanza* project still went into production, with fellow Canadian John Ireland playing the role of Ben's brother, Captain Aaron Cartwright. It was hoped that a new series could be developed, but without the original Cartwright clan, who had become almost family to most TV viewers over the age of 14, no one seemed interested.

Perhaps Michael Landon best summed up the feelings of Pa Cartwright's millions of fans when he eulogized: "I never stopped seeing Lorne as my dad."

CHAPTER FOUR

Norma Shearer
(1902–1983)

NORMA SHEARER WAS THE EPITOME OF GLAMOUR DURING her glory days in Hollywood. There were few films in which she appeared that did not maximize her beauty and poise, yet despite her physical elegance, Norma possessed a true acting talent that earned her five Oscar nominations by 1936.

But, as with many other cinema stars of her generation, Norma Shearer has perhaps become a forgotten film legend. She shone brightly, if briefly compared to such cinema contemporaries as Joan Crawford and Greta Garbo, as one of Tinseltown's most celebrated silent film performers. But as she entered the sound era of motion pictures, her output decreased sharply, though most of the films she made during this period have become certified classics.

Yet as genuine as was Norma Shearer's stardom, so was her place in Hollywood society. Her marriage to movie mogul Irving Thalberg secured her an exalted spot among the film community's elite, and following Thalberg's premature passing, she was frequently seen escorted by such well-known personages of the time as George Raft.

Unlike many show business personalities who desperately cling onto their former fame well past their prime, Norma abandoned her career while she was still in demand for film roles, choosing instead to concentrate on being a wife and mother. But even though retired from the limelight, she was responsible for launching the careers of Janet Leigh and actor-turned-producer Robert Evans (who, on Norma's recommendation, played Irving Thalberg in the 1957 Lon Chaney film biography *Man of a Thousand Faces*).

The future "First Lady of MGM" began life as Edith Norma Shearer on August 11, 1902, in West-mount, Québec. Norma was named after her mother, Edith Fisher Shearer. Her father, Andrew, was a general contractor and construction company executive, whose factory was the first to manufacture hockey sticks.

Norma and her two older siblings, sister Athole and brother Douglas (who would go on to achieve behind-the-screen success at MGM as a 12-time Academy Award–winning sound director), were raised in comfortable surroundings on Grosvenor Street, located in one of the most exclusive neigh-bourhoods of Montréal.

From a young age, Norma was a fan of the movies. Her favourite screen performer was Pearl White, who had become world famous for her *Perils of Pauline* series. Norma decided that she wanted to emulate the star, and at age 14, entered a beauty contest and won.

At the close of World War I, her father's construction business suffered in the post-war economy. This change in the family's economic situation forced Norma to quit school at age 16 and go to work selling sheet music. The financial stress affected the Shearer's marriage, and in 1920, Edith Shearer separated from her husband and moved with Athole and Norma to New York. She hoped her daughters, with their striking good looks, might pursue careers in modelling or the theatre.

In the meantime, to earn a living, Edith worked at a department store, while Athole and Norma haunted the casting offices of Broadway looking for their big break. Norma was finally able to arrange a meeting with the famed Florenz Ziegfeld, producer of *The Ziegfeld Follies*. But Ziegfeld turned Norma down. In his opinion, her legs were too short, her teeth needed straightening, and her eye had a cast that gave her a cross-eyed look. Later in her career, she had this physical defect corrected and, like many other stars of the time, had her teeth capped. By her own admission, she wasn't particularly fond of her legs, an attitude perhaps engendered by Ziegfeld's criticism.

Norma was dejected by her interview with Ziegfeld, but she was not discouraged. She remembered Pearl White and thought of the movies as her next option. Norma had spunk, and when she auditioned for D.W. Griffith of the Biograph Company, she made it a point to be noticed during auditions. She would either cough or shuffle her feet to bring attention to herself. These manoeuvres had the desired result, and Norma soon found herself cast as an extra in the silent film *The Sign on the Door* (1920) and later in that same year played another extra role in Griffith's *Way Down East.*

Norma's movie career certainly wasn't progressing as she had hoped, and so she returned to modelling, her face soon becoming prominent on various magazine covers, both in photographs and in illustrations. She also accepted representation by a talent agent named Edward Small. Through him, Norma obtained roles in such early pictures as *The Stealers* (1920) and *The Leather Pushers* (1922). However meagre these parts were, Norma was beginning to attract an audience. Perhaps her most prominent professional admirer was the general manager at Universal Studios, the youthful but chronically ill Irving Thalberg. Irving had been crowned the "boy genius" of Hollywood, and he was one of the 36 founders (along with Mary Pickford and Douglas Fairbanks) of the Academy of Motion Picture Arts and Sciences. Unfortunately, his was destined not to be a lengthy career. Plagued by a rheumatic heart condition, Thalberg had spent most of his boyhood bedridden and was not expected to live a long life.

Despite his efforts, Thalberg was unable to sign Norma to a Universal contract—apparently the studio was unwilling to cover the moving expenses for Norma, her mother and sister (who would later go on to marry famed director Howard Hawks). But the situation improved when Thalberg moved over to the newly incorporated MGM studios. There Norma was given an important role as Consuelo in the Lon Chaney classic *He Who Gets Slapped* (1924). From that point on, Norma's career progressed. She signed a six-month contract at a pay rate of $150 per week, which *did* include moving expenses for herself, her mother and her sister.

MGM was the studio where Norma Shearer would achieve her fame. While her film career initially continued with small roles in such pictures as *His Secretary* (1925) and *The Devil's Circus* (1926), Irving Thalberg gradually groomed her for more prominent parts.

Finally, the impatient young actress was given the role of Kathi in *The Student Prince in Old Heidelberg* (1927). Her performance in the film duly impressed MGM president Louis B. Mayer—and Thalberg. Shortly after filming was completed, Irving and Norma became engaged. However, even though L.B. Mayer thought of Irving Thalberg as a son, he strongly advised Norma against marrying Irving because of his prognosis for a short life. Not many actors would dare to defy Mayer, undoubtedly the most powerful man in Hollywood. But Norma did, and she and Irving were married in September 1929. During their two-year engagement, Norma converted to Irving's Jewish faith.

Because of her marriage to Thalberg, Norma was treated like a queen on the MGM lot. Joan Crawford, also under contract to the studio, once remarked: "How can I compete with her when she's sleeping with the boss."

Her first film roles upon returning to MGM were *The Latest from Paris* and *The Actress,* both released in 1928. Norma made her debut in sound films the following year when she appeared in *The Trial of Mary Dugan.* She received good reviews for her role and easily made the transition to talkies.

With her next film, *The Last of Mrs. Cheyney* (1929), Norma began playing the type of society role for which she would become best known. The following year, she won a Best Actress Academy Award for her role as Jerry Bernard Martin in *The Divorcee.* In her acceptance speech, she said: "I wish to take this glorious opportunity to express my deep affection and admiration for all those wonderful people in the motion picture business it has been my privilege to know and admire and to call my friends throughout the years."

On the personal front, on August 25, 1930, Norma gave birth to her first child, a son named Irving Thalberg Jr. Five years later, she delivered a daughter, Katherine. Life was good for Norma as she pursued a wide range of interests and socialized grandly with the likes of Louis B. Mayer and other Hollywood notables. However, her happiness was often clouded by her concern for her husband's health.

Despite motherhood, she continued to work and appeared in a number of classic films. She received Academy Award nominations for playing a reckless society girl in love with gangster Clark Gable in *A Free Soul* (1931), Elizabeth Barrett in *The Barretts of Wimpole Street* (1934), Juliet to Leslie Howard's Romeo in *Romeo and Juliet* (1936) and the title character in the MGM extravaganza *Marie Antoinette* (1938), which also featured a young Tyrone Power and an alcohol-ravaged John Barrymore.

But two weeks after the release of *Romeo and Juliet*, on September 14, 1936, Irving Thalberg died at the age of 37 of lobular pneumonia. At his funeral, Rabbi Magnin said: "The love of Norma Shearer and Irving Thalberg was a love greater than the greatest motion picture I have ever seen, *Romeo and Juliet*."

Devastated by the expected but sudden death of her husband, Norma became ill with bronchial pneumonia. When she recovered, she considered retiring from movies, but she had a contractual commitment to appear in *Marie Antoinette*. Later, she relented her decision to retire and signed a two-year contract with MGM calling for six films at $150,000 per picture.

While every important female star in Hollywood coveted the role of Scarlett O'Hara in *Gone With the Wind* (1939), Norma was directly offered the part, but rejected it, wryly explaining: "Scarlett O'Hara is going to be a thankless and difficult role. The part I'd like to play is Rhett Butler."

Instead she appeared in *Idiot's Delight* (where she *did* work with Clark Gable) and her last classic film, *The Women*, in which she co-starred with real-life rival Joan Crawford, as well as with Joan Fontaine and Paulette Goddard (the latter two had also tested for the Scarlett O'Hara role). Although Mary Haines was Norma's final important role, it was arguably Joan Crawford who stole the show with her role of the bitchy home wrecker.

On the personal front, Norma was often seen around town in the company of Warner Brothers tough guy George Raft. Many assumed that theirs was a serious affair, but Norma was not ready to remarry, and Raft was unable to since he could not obtain a divorce from his long-estranged wife, whom he had married in the 1920s. Norma's boss, L.B. Mayer, personally did not approve of the well-publicized relationship, stating: "A nice Jewish girl like Norma should not be seen with a roughneck like that." Despite their attraction to one another, Norma and George eventually drifted apart.

Norma still remained a popular draw among theatregoers, but her final films were a forgettable lot. What is unfortunate is that Norma, with her penchant for choosing superior material, passed on both *Now, Voyageur* (inherited by Bette Davis) and

Mrs. Miniver (which won Greer Garson an Oscar). Norma closed out her MGM contract and her career with *Her Cardboard Lover* (1942), a tired romantic comedy co-starring Robert Taylor.

Norma never officially announced her retirement, but she permanently made the decision after meeting and marrying Sun Valley ski instructor and real estate promoter Martín Arrouge, who was 20 years her junior. Despite the age difference, their marriage was a happy one. In fact, Norma gave up her Jewish faith for that of Roman Catholicism. She remained active, raising her family and socializing with a close circle of friends.

Sadly, when she was in her mid-70s, she was diagnosed with Alzheimer's disease, eventually leading her family to make the difficult decision to have her transferred to the Motion Picture Retirement Home, where she passed away on June 12, 1983.

"The First Lady of MGM" was laid to rest at Forest Lawn in the Great Mausoleum, Sanctuary of Benediction, in Glendale, California.

CHAPTER FIVE

Glenn Ford
(1916–)

GLENN FORD HAS ENJOYED AN INCREDIBLE CAREER, AND while no longer active in the industry owing to poor health, he can look back with satisfaction on his many film accomplishments. He has appeared in 110 movies, a number of which have become cinema classics. Yet remarkably, even with roles in *Gilda* (1946), *The Big Heat* (1953) and most especially *Blackboard Jungle* (1955), he has never even been nominated for an Academy Award.

But Glenn Ford himself remains modest about his career. When asked by an interviewer which of his movies was his favourite, Glenn replied that he didn't have one and that rather than watching his films, he would prefer to spend time at the beach.

Modesty aside, Glenn Ford was one of the biggest stars that Hollywood ever produced, especially during his peak decade, the 1950s, when he starred in an amazing number of quality productions. While, as with other stars of his era, his career waned during the 1960s, he still remained a well-liked and respected member of the film industry and continued to appear in starring roles, though in lesser productions.

Perhaps one of the reasons for Glenn Ford's
success was that audiences could identify with
him. His characters rarely, if ever, were given
larger-than-life dimensions, *à la* John Wayne.
Certainly he played his share of heroes, but his
characters were ordinary people who became
heroic through circumstances thrust upon them,
and he remained modest as the actor himself.
Glenn was quoted as saying: "I've never played
anyone but myself onscreen."

True, but that encompasses a lot of admirable
qualities including, truth, honesty, strength and
integrity.

Gwyllyn Samuel Newton Ford was born in the
town of Portneuf, Québec, on May 1, 1916. His
birth could have been traumatic because just
weeks prior to his delivery, his 23-year-old mother,
Hannah, had been involved in a tragic house fire.
Because he entered the world without complications, Hannah would always refer her son as a
"miracle baby." Gwyllyn's father, Newton, worked
as a railway conductor on the Canadian Pacific
Railway line between Montréal and Québec City.

Gwyllyn had his first taste of acting in 1921, at
the age of five, when he was cast in a community
production of *Tom Thumb's Wedding*, and he never
forgot the experience. In 1923, the Ford family,
concerned for the health of Hannah's mother,
who had never really recovered from the fire,

moved to California, eventually settling in Santa Monica. Gwyllyn attended Santa Monica High School, where he discovered a passion for drama. After appearing in several high school productions, Gwyllyn decided that he wanted to become an actor after graduation. His father agreed to let him pursue this goal, but with the proviso that he learn some other skills in case acting didn't work out. Gwyllyn complied and quickly learned various trades, including carpentry, electronics and mechanics.

At 18, Gwyllyn landed his first professional theatre job as a stage manager and prop master. Within just a year, the eager youth graduated from extra parts to a speaking role in a West Coast travelling company's production of Lillian Hellman's *The Children's Hour.* He then toured with various companies for four years, appearing in over 50 stage roles and achieving recognition in New York, San Diego and San Francisco.

Glenn still believed his move into the business was a quirk of fate. "I never thought I would become an actor," he said. "I was told a long time ago that I wasn't the type."

It wasn't long before his talent and his clean-cut good looks were noticed by film producers, and in 1937, he made his movie debut in the Paramount short *Night in Manhattan.* A year later, he was cast by talent agent Tom Moore in his first feature, 20th Century-Fox's *Heaven with a Barbed Wire Fence.*

The film was mild fare and made little impact at the box office, but Columbia chief Harry Cohn, always searching for promising new talent that he could employ cheaply, signed Gwyllyn to a studio contract. First, though, at Cohn's insistence, Gwyllyn had to change his name. Gwyllyn complied and, rejecting Cohn's suggestions, became Glenn Ford in honour of his father's birthplace, Glenford.

The newly renamed Glenn Ford quickly entered the ranks of Columbia's B-unit group of actors. His first picture was the 63-minute *My Son is Guilty* (1939). He also played a supporting role in *Blondie Plays Cupid* (1940), part of the popular series based on the Chic Young comic strip, *Blondie*.

More noteworthy were his roles in his first A pictures *The Lady in Question* (1940), which teamed him for the first time with Rita Hayworth and director Charles Vidor, and *So Ends Our Night* (1941), in which he played Ludwig Kern, a young Jew fleeing from Nazi Germany. Both the picture and Ford were awarded critical praise, with the actor being proclaimed as "one of the best juvenile finds of the year."

He was paired for the first time with his good friend William Holden (another young Columbia acquisition, who had made his mark as the lead in 1939's *Golden Boy*) in the western *Texas* (1941). Because of the growing success of both actors, the studio afforded the picture a higher budget than usual. Glenn would later recall that right from the start he and Holden were always competing with one another, yet that never dampened their friendship.

"He was my best friend," Glenn would tearfully recall following Holden's tragic death in 1981. Holden, who fought an alcohol problem throughout most of his later years, fell while intoxicated, struck his head on the corner of a table and bled to death.

Glenn had other good roles in *The Adventures of Martin Eden* (1942), based on Jack London's semi-autobiographical novel, the western *The Desperadoes* (1943) and *Destroyer* (1943), with Edward G. Robinson.

However, with World War II in full swing, Glenn halted the upward momentum of his movie career to enlist in the Marine Corps, where he served from 1943 to 1945 on both the Pacific and Atlantic fronts. Among his many wartime endeavours, he helped construct safe houses in France for those hiding from the Nazis.

Glenn served with distinction during the war, both with the navy and the marines. He was one of the first to enter the Dachau extermination camp following its liberation. His military contribution was duly noted, and he was later appointed commander in the Naval Reserves. In 1992, Glenn Ford was awarded the Legion d'Honneur medal for his courageous service during World War II. His other commendations include the Medal of Honour, presented by the veterans of foreign wars, the Medaille de la France Libre for the liberation of France, two medals from the U.S. Navy and the Vietnamese Legion of Merit for the two tours of duties he served with the 3rd Marine Amphibious Force. Glenn holds the distinction of being the only actor to have served with both the Green Berets and the French Foreign Legion.

While on leave in 1943, Glenn married actress and dancer Eleanor Powell. His only child, a son named Peter, was born in 1945. Glenn now had a family to support, but initially his prospects of returning to film work were not encouraging. He, like pal Bill Holden and others, had returned to an industry that had changed during their absence. Glenn's career, which had seemed so promising prior to the war, now looked to be virtually over.

Discouraged, he considered accepting an offer from Howard Hughes' Lougheed Company. But his fortunes changed when Bette Davis, admiring of servicemen and respecting of Glenn's talents, spotted Glenn having lunch at the Warner Brothers commissary and requested him for her leading man in her upcoming picture *A Stolen Life* (1946). The studio had wanted contract player Robert Alda (father of Alan) for the role, but Bette stood firm. The success of that film, and especially the sizzling noir classic *Gilda* (filmed after the Davis movie but released 45 days earlier) put Glenn's career firmly back on track. In *Gilda*, he played Johnny Farrell, the employee of casino boss George Macready, who begins an affair with Macready's wife, leading to tragic consequences. In the picture, Glenn was re-teamed with director Charles Vidor and his favourite leading lady Rita Hayworth.

With just these two films, Glenn had once again become one of Columbia's most valuable properties. In 1948, he co-starred again with Hayworth in the period piece *The Loves of Carmen*. Then he was paired with his friend William Holden in the psychological western *The Man from Colorado*. Glenn gave a strong villainous performance as Colonel Owen Devereaux, a mentally unhinged judge who rules his territory through fear and tyranny.

In pictures such as this, Glenn proved his versatility. He was equally adept at comedy or drama and so was kept busy with a variety of challenging roles. In 1949, for example, he played a treasury agent on the trail of an Al Capone–like mobster in the noir crime thriller *The Undercover Man*, a prospector based on the true-life Jacob Walz (the "Dutchman" for whom the famous Arizona "Lost Dutchman Mines" was named) in *Lust for Gold* and an idealistic young physician in *The Doctor and the Girl*.

Glenn's dedication to his craft led to his receiving the Golden Apple Award in 1948 for "Most Cooperative Actor." Earlier, his alma mater, Santa Monica High School, honoured Glenn by naming the school's top acting award after him.

Glenn really hit his stride as he entered his second decade of film acting. Because of the collapse of the studio system and the advent of television,

the careers of more established actors were beginning to decline while Glenn was about to enter the
busiest stage of his career.

However, though he was active, Glenn's films
during the early 1950s were mainly undistin-
guished. Two exceptions were the 1951 biography
of golfer Ben Hogan, *Follow the Sun*, and *The Man
from the Alamo* (1953). That same year, he had a big
hit with Fritz Lang's *The Big Heat*, in which he
played Dave Bannion, a vengeance-minded detective on the trail of his wife's killers, most notably
a gangland assassin played by a young Lee Marvin.

Suddenly, Glenn's career shifted into high gear.
In 1954, the legendary Fritz Lang directed him
again in the murder mystery *Human Desire*. But it
was his role of inner-city schoolteacher Richard
Dadier in Richard Brooks' *Blackboard Jungle* (1955)
that was really the highlight of his career. Dadier
(or Daddy-O, as he is contemptuously called by his
rebellious students, including a young Sidney
Poitier and pre-*M*A*S*H* Jamie Farr) at first tries
to reason with his class, but as the situation
becomes increasingly threatening both to the
teacher and his wife (Anne Francis), Dadier's calm
demeanour finally explodes in a dynamic class-
room confrontation. It was a complex role of transition for which Glenn surely should have been
considered for an Oscar nomination.

However, the picture did keep him on Hollywood's A list. His other notable films of the 1950s

included the suspense drama *Ransom!* (1956) and *The Teahouse of the August Moon* with Marlon Brando impersonating a Japanese.

Glenn possessed an adventurous streak that was perhaps best exemplified by his performance in *The White Tower* (1950). He was the only actor ever to climb Mont Blanc, Europe's highest mountain. As Glenn later said: "The one thing I learned from that experience was that it's more difficult to go down a mountain than to go up."

His roles in westerns probably made the greatest overall audience impact during the decade. He admitted that these were his favourite parts to play. Indeed, half of his Hollywood pictures were in the western genre. He'd learned to ride a horse as a teenager while working in the stables at Will Rogers' ranch, and he certainly looked comfortable in cowboy clothes. What many fans do not know is that Glenn was credited with being the fastest draw in Hollywood. He could draw and fire his gun within 0.4 seconds, topping both James Arness (*Gunsmoke*) and even John Wayne. The Canadian from Québec became one of the most recognized and authentic western stars of the day.

Glenn's contribution to the genre has been considerable, including heroic roles in *Jubal* (1956), *The Fastest Gun Alive* (1956) and *Cowboy* (1958), along with a villainous turn opposite Van Heflin in *3:10 to Yuma* (1957).

His work in the field resulted in his 1978 induction into the National Cowboy Hall of Fame by the Western Heritage Museum.

But Glenn's effective portrayals as a cowboy did not come without a price. During one of his westerns, Glenn was kicked in the right side of his jaw by a horse, damaging his face, with Glenn thereafter insisting that he be photographed looking to camera left.

Unfortunately, come the close of the 1950s, Glenn's personal life was not faring so well, either. Although he enjoyed romantic relationships with Evelyn Ankers, Joan Crawford, Brigitte Bardot, Connie Stevens and Debbie Reynolds, his 16-year union with Eleanor Powell had dissolved. Later marriages to Kathryn Hays (1966–69), Cynthia Hayward (1977, divorce date not available) and Jeanne Baus (1993–94) fared no better. Glenn has always maintained that his dearest love was Rita Hayworth, who was his neighbour in Hollywood. Speaking of their onscreen teamings, Glenn admitted: "We were terribly fond of one another. I guess that electricity came across onscreen. I really was in love with Rita."

Glenn admitted his personal shortcomings in a perceptive 1949 interview: "We are all three people. The person we think we are. The person the world thinks we are. And the person we really are."

During the 1960s, Glenn racked up some impressive screen credits. Perhaps his three most memorable roles were as bootleg racketeer Dave "the Dude" Conway in Frank Capra's *Pocketful of Miracles* (1961), for which he received top billing over Bette Davis, playboy-turned-resistance-fighter Julio Desnoyers in *Four Horsemen of the Apocalypse* (1962), FBI agent John Ripley in *Experiment in Terror* (1962) and widower Tom Corbett in *The Courtship of Eddie's Father* (1963), which co-starred a young Ronnie Howard as his son.

As the 1960s progressed and Glenn's movie career was winding down, he began venturing into television. He starred in the critically acclaimed made-for-television movie *The Brotherhood of the Bell* (1970) before lending his presence to two short-lived TV series, *Cade's County* (1971–72) and *The Family Holvak* (1975). *The Family Holvak* was a series prequel to the TV film *The Greatest Gift* (1974), in which Glenn's character, Reverend Tom Holvak, is killed while trying to prevent a robbery. Glenn's talents were further put to use in roles in the acclaimed miniseries *The Sacketts* (1979), *Beggarman, Thief* (1979) and *Once an Eagle* (1980).

His later film credits included the Sensurround production *Midway* (1976) and a brief, poignant performance as Clark Kent's adopted father in *Superman* (1978). Glenn even returned to Canada to play the soon-to-be-murdered psychiatrist in the horror thriller *Happy Birthday to Me* (1981). His last feature role was in *Border Shootout* (1990).

In 1970, Glenn published his memoir *Glenn Ford R.F.D. Beverly Hills,* which deals primarily with his many environmental concerns. Soon to come, however, will be his autobiography, co-authored by son Peter.

Glenn returned to military service during the Vietnam War. While well past the age of active service, Glenn bravely served his adopted country during this controversial conflict.

Although Glenn became an American citizen in 1939, he retains a strong pride in being Canadian. In a television interview, Glenn once admitted that he was not ashamed to shed a tear each time he heard the Canadian anthem played. Perhaps this is not so strange, considering that he is related to Sir John A. Macdonald, the first prime minister of Canada. However, he also retains an American connection, as he is a direct descendant of President Martin Van Buren.

Regarding his Everyman image, Glenn stated: "When I'm on camera, I have to do things pretty much the way I do things in everyday life. It gives the audience someone real to identify with."

This statement provides a wonderful summation of Glenn Ford's talents. From real-life war veteran to adventurer to movie hero, Glenn Ford today enjoys a much-deserved and appreciated quiet life, residing with son Peter, daughter-in-law Lynda and two of his grandchildren in Beverly Hills. This former movie hero passes his time gardening and often communicating with his fans on the Internet.

CHAPTER SIX

Fay Wray
(1907–2004)

FAY WRAY WAS THE QUINTESSENTIAL SCREAM QUEEN. Regardless of her other cinematic achievements, she will unquestionably always be best known for her roles in horror movies—most particularly as the object of the giant simian's affections in the classic 1933 adventure thriller *King Kong*. She never truly became a star, but because of her role in *Kong*, Fay is probably better remembered today than many other more popular female stars of the era. Long before Jamie Lee Curtis was menaced by Michael Myers in *Halloween* and fellow Canadian Neve Campbell was stalked by the masked killer in *Scream*, Fay Wray set the standard for which all of her successors owe her a debt of gratitude.

Whether threatened by the questionable intentions of the mighty ape of Skull Island, or more directly menaced by the diabolical impulses of co-star Lionel Atwill in her early films, Fay screamed…and survived. She never made it through to the end credits solely because of her own fortitude, simply because that was just not how things were done in those days. There had to be a handsome hero on hand to save the damsel

in distress. And Fay always had plenty of leading men ready to rescue her from her plight. A sampling includes Bruce Cabot, Lee Tracy and Melvyn Douglas. Later, after she had shifted away from horror roles, she could count among her rescuers tough guys George Raft and Alan Ladd.

But her movies outside the horror genre are mostly a forgotten lot. Who today remembers pictures with the titles *Cheating Cheaters* (1934) or *Melody for Three* (1941)?

So, for better or for worse, Fay Wray will forever be remembered as the first "mistress of the macabre."

Vina Fay Wray's beginnings certainly did not put her on the pathway to her future movie destiny. She was born on September 15, 1907, on the outskirts of Cardston, Alberta. Her parents were Joseph Herber and Vina Marguerite Jones Wray, who married on December 16, 1910, in Brandon, Manitoba. Vina was the fourth of six children born to the Wray family, following Joseph, Vaida and Willow, and preceding Richard and Victor. The family relocated to Arizona in June 1911, then moved to Utah, where Vina spent most of her childhood. There were escalating tensions in the marriage, and when Joseph Wray took a job in the nearby town of Bingham, Utah, he never returned to the family. Young Vina saw him only a few times after that.

Sadly, the separation of her parents left the Wray clan in desperate financial straits. Their difficulties were further compounded by the influenza epidemic of 1918, which resulted in the death of Vina's older sister Vaida. Vina, whose own health was fragile, left for the better climate of California when she was 14, because her mother didn't want her to endure another long, cold winter. Vina travelled to Los Angeles with a companion named William Mortensen, a friend of her sister Willow. He found a series of families to take her in, and she started junior high school, where she was popular and earned high grades. William worked in a photography studio (he eventually went on to become a well-respected art photographer), and Fay often posed for him. One day, she jokingly struck a sexy pose and later sent the picture to her mother, who, certain that her daughter was being compromised, quickly came to Los Angeles.

It didn't take long for the attractive girl to make her mark in motion pictures. Dropping her first name, Fay made her debut as an extra in a comedy short in 1914. Gradually, she secured enough of a reputation to be hired by Hal Roach to play lead roles in his one-reelers. From her work with Roach, she was hired by Universal to appear in a series of two-reel westerns, soon graduating to five-reelers and co-playing with Hoot Gibson. In 1926, for example, she appeared in eight pictures, with such unmemorable titles as *Don Key (A Son of Burro)*, *Don't Shoot* and *Lazy Lightning*.

Fay's appearances in these "oaters" resulted in the Western Association of Motion Picture Advertisers selecting her as one of 13 young starlets most likely to succeed in movies. She was chosen along with Janet Gaynor and Mary Astor as candidates for stardom. Obviously, the Association had a shrewd eye for talent.

Of course, the westerns in which she appeared were cheap B and even C productions and not films in which one really had the chance to display true acting ability. But they did bring Fay to the attention of director Erich von Stroheim, who was preparing to film *The Wedding March* (1928), the picture that securely affirmed von Stroheim as one of Hollywood's most acclaimed directors. As for his casting of Fay Wray in the leading role, he stated: "As soon as I had seen Fay Wray and spoken to her for a few minutes, I knew I had found the right girl. I didn't even have to take a test of her. Fay has spirituality, but she also has that very real sex appeal that takes hold of the hearts of men."

The Wedding March is still regarded as a cinematic masterpiece, despite its rather simplistic plot about an Austrian prince, Nicholaus von Wildeliebe-Rauffenburg (von Stroheim), who agrees to marry for money and position to assist his family, whose fortunes have diminished. Instead, the prince falls in love with the beautiful but poor Mitzi Schrammell (Wray).

Her appearance in this picture brought Fay Wray to the attention of the moviegoing public. In a press release distributed to *Motion Picture* magazine, Harry Carr, co-writer of *The Wedding March* script with von Stroheim, called Fay "one of the most remarkable personalities I have ever known in the movies."

Fay herself always referred to *The Wedding March* as her favourite picture and regarded the role of Mitzi as the one part in which she most fully expressed herself as an actress. She believed that her career would have had a different quality and character had she continued to work with von Stroheim, whom she considered her favourite director.

Fay Wray's star seemed definitely on the rise. When Paramount took over the distribution of *The Wedding March*, Fay was put under contract by the studio, who promptly set her to co-star with another new acquisition, Gary Cooper, in William Wellman's *The Legion of the Condemned* (1928). The script for the movie had been written by John Monk Saunders, a World War I flying instructor and former Rhodes scholar. Attractive and charming, he was enchanted by Fay's "Nefertiti eyes," and the two embarked on a relationship.

Fay continued her association with the fast-rising Gary Cooper in *The First Kiss* (1928) and *The Texan* (1930). She performed her last silent role in *The Four Feathers* (1929), directed by Merian C. Cooper and Ernest B. Schoedsack, who had a tremendous impact on Fay's career in the next few years. The silent film star successfully made the transition to sound. Fay's voice recorded well, and she effectively used her vocal talents to play the moll Ritzy in Joseph von Sternberg's first sound feature, the gangster drama *Thunderbolt* (1929).

While she was filming *The First Kiss*, Fay received news of the death of her brother Vivien. John Monk Saunders arrived to comfort her and, with Gary Cooper acting as witness, Fay and John were married. The couple moved into a Spanish-style villa, where they entertained frequently in grand style. Their relationship had a dark underside, however, as the emotionally unstable Saunders proved to be a compulsive womanizer and periodic drunk.

Despite the couple's penchant for socializing, Fay maintained an active work schedule. Even after her contract with Paramount expired and was not renewed, Fay kept busy, appearing in 25 features and working for virtually every major Hollywood studio. Two of her better films during this period were *Dirigible* (1931), made for Columbia, and the First National gangster picture *The Finger Points* (1931), which also included Clark Gable in the cast.

In 1932, Cooper and Schoedsack offered Fay a role opposite the "tallest, darkest leading man in Hollywood." She was one of a dozen actresses that tried out for the role and was reportedly selected because she screamed the loudest. Little did Fay know that her co-star would not be either Clark

Gable or Cary Grant, but rather an 18-inch pup-
pet replete with articulated joints that Willis
O'Brien would animate onto film as a 50-foot
behemoth named *King Kong* (1933). The film had
the then astronomical budget of $680,000. Fay
was paid $10,000 on a 10-week guarantee that
stretched into 10 months for her role as Ann Darrow, the part that would guarantee her motion
picture immortality. While the movie virtually
saved RKO from bankruptcy, neither Fay nor any
other of the picture's participants ever saw another
dime from the moneymaking extravaganza. Resid-
uals and profit participation would not be considered until the establishment of the Screen Actors
Guild just a few years later.

Dracula (1930), *Frankenstein* (1931) and *The
Mummy* (1932) had all preceded the coming of
King Kong, yet his was the grandest entrance of all.
The film thundered onto movie screens with a
presence that thrilled Depression-era audiences.
And as his hapless victim, Fay evoked the sympa-
thy of moviegoers, who embraced her peril.

King Kong's bullet-riddled demise atop the
Empire State Building has become the stuff of
movie folklore. Although Fay was saved from the
mighty Kong's grasp thanks to the efficiency of
a squadron of machine-gunning biplanes, she was
in no way out of harm's way. Her next menacing
movie encounters were of the human variety, sort
of—but even more deadly.

Prior to *King Kong*, the Cooper-Schoedsack team had cast Fay in *The Most Dangerous Game* (1932), where she starred opposite Leslie Banks, who played the crazed, human-hunting Count Zarkoff. Her less threatening co-players were Joel McCrae and *King Kong* co-star Robert Armstrong.

More horror remained on the horizon. Fay had appeared as actor Lionel Atwill's daughter in *Dr. X* (1932), then played his intended victim in *Mystery of the Wax Museum* (1933), both filmed in the early

two-colour Technicolor process. She once more appeared opposite the diabolical Atwill in *The Vampire Bat* (1933).

Fay's two other 1930s genre films were the supernatural voodoo drama *Black Moon* (1934) and the British-made *The Clairvoyant* (aka *The Evil Mind*), starring opposite Claude Rains, who played a phoney mind reader who discovers that perhaps his powers do transcend into the psychic world.

Fay's contribution to horror cinema, while impressive, did not leave her entirely out of mainstream movies. Among her other noteworthy roles during the 1930s were *The Bowery* (1933), in which she co-starred with Wallace Beery, George Raft and the young Jackie Cooper, *The Affairs of Cellini* (1934) with Fredric March and *Viva Villa!* (1934), again with Wallace Beery in the title role as Pancho Villa. In fact, throughout 1933 and 1934, she began a new film every fourth Friday—standard film production procedure in those days.

There were some letdowns, however. Fay was disappointed when she lost the part of the female lead opposite Spencer Tracy (whom she very much admired and had co-starred with in the forgettable film, *Shanghai Madness*) in *Man's Castle* (1933) to Loretta Young, and later the part of Maria (played by Margo) in *Lost Horizon* (1937).

Fay's career peaked in the mid-1930s. Following her film successes during that period, she was again relegated to a series of unmemorable B pictures with such titles as *Come Out of the Pantry* (1935), *When Knights Were Bold* (1936) and *Murder in Greenwich Village* (1937).

Actually, Fay received more publicity for her personal life than her film career. Although she and John Monk Saunders had become the parents of a baby girl, Susan, the couple divorced in 1938. Tragically, the unstable Saunders committed suicide in 1940 while Fay was in rehearsal for the play *Margin for Error.*

But Fay again discovered happiness when she met and married Academy Award–winning screenwriter Robert Riskin in 1942. While Fay's career was definitely on the decline during the 1940s—she only appeared in four forgettable films throughout the decade—she devoted herself to her husband and family (she had two more children, Bobby and Victoria, with Riskin). However, when Riskin suffered a debilitating stroke in the early 1950s, a decline in income and escalating medical bills required that Fay return to work, although both her roles and the quality of the films in which she was seen did nothing to enhance her career. After Riskin died in 1955, Fay again reduced her workload. She appeared only intermittently onscreen in such pictures as *The Cobweb* (1955), directed by Vincente Minelli and co-starring Richard Widmark and Lillian Gish, *Queen Bee* (1955) with Joan Crawford, and, perhaps most notably, the gangster thriller *Hell on Frisco Bay* (1955) with Alan Ladd and Edward G. Robinson.

Prior to her retirement from the screen, Fay lent her talents to such films as *Rock, Pretty Baby* (1956), *Crime of Passion* (1957), in which she co-played opposite fellow Canadian Raymond Burr, and perhaps the nadir of her career, *Dragstrip Riot* (1958). She did, however, receive good critical reviews for her role as Mrs. Brent in *Tammy and the Bachelor* (1957).

Fay also did her share of television, showing up in guest roles on such popular programs as *Studio 57, General Electric Theater, Kraft Television Theater, Perry Mason* and *Wagon Train*. She also appeared as 16-year-old Natalie Wood's mother in the series *The Pride of the Family* (1953).

Fay's professional career wound down when she found romance with Dr. Sanford Rothenberg, who had been Riskin's neurosurgeon during the years of his illness. The couple wed in 1970.

Though retired, Fay kept herself active, penning her autobiography, *On the Other Hand,* in 1989. Her last onscreen role was in the 1980 television movie *Gideon's Trumpet,* opposite Henry Fonda. After her husband's death in 1991, Fay maintained an active lifestyle through public appearances. Unlike Greta Garbo, Fay kept herself accessible to her fans and admirers, at the age of 90 becoming a frequent sight driving her own car or appearing at theatre openings or screenings of her films. Perhaps her most prominent appearance came in conjunction with her testimony before Congress concerning royalties owed to screenwriters and their heirs before 1960.

Fay was present at the opening of her play *The Meadowlark,* in August 1997, an autobiographical presentation that was staged at the Barnstormers Summer Theater in Tamworth, New Hampshire, and directed by her daughter Susan. Toward the end of her life she made few public appearances, but in 1998 she accompanied her good friend Gloria Stuart to the Academy Awards presentations, where Gloria was up for an Oscar for Best Actress for her role in *Titanic.* Her last public appearance was in June 2004 at the premiere of the documentary *Broadway: The Golden Ages,* directed by close friend Rick McKay.

Fay Wray passed away at her Manhattan apartment at the age of 97 on August 8, 2004.

The actress regarded her film career philosophically: "I would have loved to have had more roles of more unusual character and depth, and I often thought that was too bad. However, it's a strange thing. I think I have at least one film that people have cared enough about to make them feel good. I think it's a strange kind of magic that *King Kong* has. People who have seen it—their lives have been changed because of it, and they have told me so."

A personal remembrance by Dr. Philip Chamberlin, former officer of the Academy of Motion Picture Arts and Sciences and now president of the National Arts Foundation:

Hal Wallis introduced me to Fay Wray at a reception held at the Los Angeles County Museum of Art in 1970, when I was head of the museum's Film Department. Fay's warmth and intelligence exerted a powerful attraction for me and despite her being about 18 years my senior, I was strongly tempted to abandon my love, Mary Lindsay, and make a play for Fay. Fortunately, I avoided making

Fay Wray and Dr. Philip Chamberlin

a fool of myself, and it was more than enough that Fay and I became fast friends.

A year or so later, I borrowed Jack L. Warner's personal nitrate print of *Mystery of the Wax Museum* that was then the only known print of the film to survive. What a revelation it was to see the original beauty of its two-strip Technicolor process with dazzling flame oranges and blue-green hues, masterfully utilized by Director Michael Curtiz and his cameraman Ray Rennahan, to enhance the psychological progress of the plot! Any study of film aesthetics would be immensely enriched by a careful examination of this film, the last two-colour masterpiece produced in Hollywood.

Alas, copies struck from the preservation negative that we made do no justice to the subtleties of the original print, now lost forever in time. And for those whose familiarity with Fay Wray's work goes no further than her star turn in *King Kong*, her luminous presence in this stunningly beautiful movie is likewise dimmed, rather like seeing a magazine photo of Van Gogh's "Starry Night" against viewing the original painting in a museum setting.

When I organized the first Los Angeles Film Exposition (Filmex) in the fall of 1971, Fay consented to make a rare public appearance to introduce *Mystery of the Wax Museum* (again using Jack Warner's mint-condition original print). Despite scheduling the showing at midnight on Friday, November 12, 1971, the 1492 seats of Grauman's

Chinese Theatre were quickly sold out. I presented Fay to the wildly enthusiastic audience, and she was surprised, exhilarated and genuinely moved by the standing ovation she received.

Two years later, when a visiting film critic from Paris, Jean Domarchi, arrived in Los Angeles with a request to meet Fay Wray, I called Fay and set up an appointment. We arrived at Fay's Century City apartment by mid-afternoon so that Domarchi could deliver an important message from Erich von Stroheim, who had asked Domarchi that if he ever went to Los Angeles to please convey his most sincere and highest regards to the actress he most respected of all he had worked with. Erich von Stroheim had, of course, sought out Fay Wray for the lead in his master-piece *The Wedding March*, and was now, in a sense, speaking to Fay from beyond the grave (von Stroheim had died in Paris some 16 years before). Fay was overcome with emotion and burst into tears because, as she explained, von Stroheim meant more to her than any other director she had worked with. He had taught her invaluable lessons about acting, elevated her from bit parts in minor films to stardom in a critically acclaimed work of art, introduced her to Hollywood's socially elite and had an intimate working relationship with Fay that surpassed the usual.

Fay never forgot von Stroheim, nor shall we ever forget her.

CHAPTER SEVEN

Raymond Burr
(1917–1993)

IT IS HIGHLY UNLIKELY THAT ANY OTHER TELEVISION PERFORMER has ever become so identified with a role as Raymond Burr became with Perry Mason. So strong was his association with the character that when CBS later tried to revitalize the series with light lead Monte Markham essaying the role, the attempt came to a fast halt.

Raymond would achieve further small-tube fame as the wheelchair-bound private investigator Robert Ironside, in the series *Ironside*. And of course, he enjoyed a busy film career as probably one of the movie's nastiest bad guys, cast in a series of villainous roles because of his large build and rather menacing appearance. But, despite his myriad other accomplishments, he will surely be forever remembered as TV's quintessential criminal attorney.

There were never any grey areas when it came to defining Perry Mason's public life. It was all black and white. He was the good guy—the dedicated defender whose belief in his clients' innocence would always get them acquitted, while at the same time uncovering the motivations of the true murderer.

But viewers really never got much of a chance to know Perry Mason, the man. So it was with Raymond Burr. There was always a distinct separation between Raymond's professional and private lives—one exposed to the public, the other a closely guarded secret. Perhaps that is why he was so effective in playing the role. He, too, had established a line of demarcation between his public and personal self. He rarely spoke about himself beyond his craft, and when he did offer glimpses into his private world, they were exactly that—glimpses that provided little insight except for a tendency to embellish his life, including romantic involvements and at least two marriages that apparently never existed. Another point of controversy was that he frequently mentioned a son who had died prematurely (for whom no record can be found). These embellishments make it difficult to separate fact from fiction.

However, the reason for this subterfuge can perhaps be found in Raymond's later years when, even as he was dying, he'd apparently finally found peace and contentment with a male companion.

What is most unfortunate is that embellishments were unnecessary, since Raymond's career and personal kindness stood on their own merit. Beloved by friends and fans, Raymond Burr will best be remembered as a talented, hard-working professional who remained dedicated to his craft until the end of his life.

Raymond William Stacy Burr was born on May 21, 1917, in New Westminster, British Columbia. His father was a trade agent, and the family travelled frequently, at one point temporarily settling in China. When the family returned to Canada in 1923, Raymond's parents divorced, and Raymond and his younger brother and sister moved with their mother to Vallejo, California, where they lived with their grandparents. During this time, Raymond's mother supported her children by playing the organ in churches and movie theatres.

Because Raymond was a large boy, he went to work at an early age, taking on a succession of odd jobs, including working as a ranch hand, deputy sheriff, forest service fire guard, photograph salesman and even a nightclub singer!

All the while he was toiling in unrewarding roughneck trades to help his family survive, Raymond dreamed of becoming an actor. Finally, at the age of 19, he met film director Anatole Litvak, who managed to get Raymond acting work with a Toronto summer stock theatre. He later joined a touring English repertory company, where he claimed to have met his first wife, Annette Sutherland, with whom he reported they'd had a son, Michael Evan Burr.

Raymond's personal relationships are shrouded in controversy. When questioned by reporters and interviewers about his relationships, Raymond would respond that his wife was killed in the same plane crash that took the life of actor Leslie Howard and that his son died of leukemia in 1953. No concrete evidence of either event can be found. There is, however, evidence to support his claim of a second marriage to Isabella Ward, which ended in divorce, while his third "wife," Laura Andrina Morgan, was said to have died of cancer in 1955. Following these tragedies, Raymond reported he preferred to remain a bachelor, which he did till the end of his life.

While it is true that Raymond attended the famed Pasadena Playhouse (where he also served a term as director), he also claimed to have taken adult education classes at Stanford and Columbia Universities, as well as the University of Chungking. But apparently these credentials have never been verified. He did, however, make his Broadway debut in 1941 in *Crazy with the Heat*, followed in 1943 by *Duke in Darkness*.

That same year, the 26-year-old Raymond put his acting ambitions on hold to enlist in the navy during World War II. He served for two years before being shot in the stomach at Okinawa and subsequently discharged.

When Raymond recovered from his injuries, he moved to Hollywood, where he began making the rounds of casting agents, only to be told that at 340 pounds he was too overweight for the movies. The motion picture business already had an economy-sized character player named Laird Cregar and obviously didn't see the need for another.

Undeterred, Raymond put himself on a six-month diet, eating just 750 calories a day. By the end of the diet, he had lost 130 pounds, and at 210 pounds, the 6'1" Raymond made his unbilled film debut as Claudette Colbert's dancing partner in *Without Reservations* (1946). But it would be his next role that would set the pattern for much of Raymond's movie career. In *San Quentin* (1946), he played Jeff Torrance, a criminal cohort of the film's main heavy, Barton MacLane. While Raymond's part was small, his intimidating physique and dark, brooding manner made him a natural for hardcore menacing roles, and he became typecast as one of the movies' quintessential noir bad men.

Over the next 10 years, Raymond provided villainous support in several outstanding films, including *Raw Deal* (1948), *Pitfall* (1948), *A Place in the Sun* (1951), *The Blue Gardenia* (1953) and *Rear Window* (1954), in which he was memorable as the sympathetic wife murderer Lars Thorwald. He also did his share of campy B pictures. *Bride of the Gorilla* (1951), in which he played the murderous lover of Barbara Payton, is probably the most notorious.

Perhaps Raymond's best-remembered movie role was his most heroic, that of reporter Steve Martin in the inserts for the North American release of *Godzilla, King of the Monsters* (1956). The film became an instant cult classic, and Raymond became so associated with the giant reptile that he even reprised his role in the remake/sequel *Godzilla: 1985*.

While Raymond kept busy with film and television work and was even heard on the radio series *Dragnet* (1949–50), he was disappointed that he was not regarded as a "star" name in the industry. Usually, his main purpose in a film was to threaten the hero, be it George Raft, Dick Powell, Robert Mitchum or even the Marx Brothers, Dean Martin or Jerry Lewis, and then be sent off to prison or suffer a suitable demise. He desperately wanted to, if not change, then at least add a new dimension to his image, and therefore was delighted when his name was considered for the role of Matt Dillon on *Gunsmoke*. He was rejected not because of his villainous typecasting, but because the producers thought his voice was too overpowering to display the semblance of vulnerability needed for the character. John Wayne, who was the initial pick for the show but was too busy with movie offers, suggested his *Big Jim McLain* (1952) and *Hondo* (1953) co-star James Arness for the part, which proved to be inspired casting. History was made when *Gunsmoke* became the longest running TV western, from 1955–75.

Despite his disappointment at losing the *Gunsmoke* part, Raymond soon found himself in the running for TV immortality. Perhaps because he had played a convincing prosecutor in *A Place in the Sun*, Raymond was asked to test for the role of district attorney Hamilton Burger for a television series based on the character created by Erle Stanley Gardner, Perry Mason.

Raymond agreed to read for the role but, again tired of his villainous typecasting and perceiving Burger to be in that mould, only on the condition that he have a separate test for the lead part as well. The show's producer Gail Patrick Jackson had her eyes set on casting either Fred MacMurray or Efrem Zimbalist Jr. for the role of Perry Mason, but she permitted Raymond to read for both characters. When Erle Stanley Gardener saw Raymond's test for Perry Mason, he immediately knew Raymond *was* the character, and the actor was cast on the spot.

However, Raymond initially had a problem that had to be addressed. Throughout his 10 years in pictures, his weight had constantly fluctuated, with Raymond probably looking his best during the filming of *Godzilla* in 1956. While his waistline was still acceptable, it was imperative for the show's success, particularly with him as the star, that he maintain an attractive physique. Raymond later admitted that with all the perks of his new celebrity, this was often an arduous task. But he possessed determination and dedication, and throughout the series' run from 1957 through 1965, he was able to comply with the physical requirement for the role.

Portraying Perry Mason gave Raymond great creative satisfaction, but the role was often a difficult one to play. Raymond had pages of dialogue to memorize, and he also had to learn and understand complex legal jargon. He often spent the night in his dressing room at the studio instead of returning home so he could have more time to study his lines.

Perry Mason was an enormous success with both critics and TV viewers. Raymond had finally become the "man of the hour," eventually picking up three Emmy Awards during the show's eight-year run. Yet he was modest about his good fortune, referring to the show as an ensemble piece and always sharing credit with his co-stars, Barbara Hale (Della Street), William Talman (Hamilton Burger), William Hopper (Paul Drake) and Ray Collins (Lieutenant Tragg).

At the show's height, Raymond was earning a reported $1 million per episode, making him one of the highest-paid performers on television. To cap off his success, he was even awarded an honorary law doctorate from the McGeorge School of Law in Sacramento, California.

Following the cancellation of *Perry Mason* in 1965, Raymond took a brief hiatus, returning to television two years later to star in *Ironside*. This popular detective series featured Raymond as Chief Robert Ironside, confined to a wheelchair after being crippled in a shooting, but still able to solve crimes with a young investigative team doing the legwork. Raymond would go on to receive two Golden Globe nominations, but his health suffered as a result of the show. The sedentary nature of the part caused him to put on excess weight, which he retained and added to for the rest of his life. He also suffered eye damage from always having to look up at his co-stars and into the bright set lights. Still, *Ironside* was another series of which Raymond was inordinately proud, and following its cancellation, it went into syndication as *The Raymond Burr Show*.

Raymond managed to keep busy by appearing in a series of acclaimed made-for-TV movies, including *Harold Robbins' 79 Park Avenue* (1977), *The Bastard* (1978) and the epic miniseries *Centennial* (1978). One of his most notable parts was that of Pope John XXIII in *Portrait: A Man Whose Name was John* (1973).

He also returned to series television with the short-lived crime drama *Kingston: Confidential* (1977), in which he played publishing magnate R.B. Kingston, who in his spare time solves crimes with a younger group of sleuths as in *Ironside*.

Raymond did some work on the big screen, but both the projects and his roles were forgettable, a possible exception being the Canadian-made feature *Tomorrow Never Comes* (1978), a hostage drama in which he played a supporting role alongside Oliver Reed and fellow Canadian John Ireland. He also lent his familiar persona to the spoof *Airplane II: The Sequel* (1982).

At the age of 68, Raymond Burr had no dearth of work. While his film work may have been disappointing, he remained a solid fixture on television. He was signed for a *Perry Mason* TV movie,

Perry Mason Returns (1985). Sadly, Barbara Hale was the only co-star still alive from the original series, but the producers ingeniously brought in her talented actor son William Katt (best known from the horror film *Carrie* and the TV series *The Greatest American Hero*) to play late investigator Paul Drake's son, Paul Jr.

The movie proved so successful (even showcasing a by now severely corpulent Raymond Burr) that 26 TV movies were made. The final installment was *Perry Mason: The Case of the Killer Kiss* in 1993.

Raymond never lost his love of acting, but his vast wealth allowed him to indulge other pleasures. His world travels led to his purchasing a 3000-acre island in Fiji. He also bought a vineyard in Sonoma, California, where the actor took great pleasure tending the grapes that produced Cabernet Sauvignon and Cabernet Franc red wines.

Apparently, however, Raymond had never really been a well man since his original *Perry Mason* days, when he was diagnosed with a cancer that eventually penetrated his liver and ended his life on September 12, 1993.

Even as Raymond knew he was dying, he struggled to complete his final *Perry Mason* movies before saying a gentle adieu and retiring to his California estate, where he hosted "farewell" parties for his closest friends.

When Raymond Burr passed away, he reminded the world of his strong Canadian ties by having his body interred at Fraser Cemetery in his birthplace of New Westminster, BC.

The city reciprocated by establishing The Raymond Burr Performing Arts Centre in October 2000. The centre's pride in Raymond is best exemplified by having a picture of the actor somewhere on display during each performance, with a customary toast to his memory held on the first night of each production.

Although he remained an intensely private person, Raymond was known as a gentle, generous man. While filming *Mara Maru* (1952), co-star Errol Flynn told Raymond that if he died with even $10 in his pocket, he would know he hadn't lived his life correctly. Raymond always used this as his own philosophy, and he put it into effect. Stories of his kindness are legion, including how on the set of *Perry Mason* he would not accept the mistreatment of his fellow actors by pushy directors and producers, threatening to walk off the set.

However, most of Raymond's humanitarian efforts remained personal. He travelled at his own expense to visit the troops fighting in both the Korean and Vietnamese conflicts. He supported at least two dozen foster children, and was particularly generous in contributing to the financial well-being of the people who inhabited the Fiji island of Naitauba, of which he was part owner.

The artistic Raymond Burr differed greatly from the characters with whom he became identified during his early movie career, roles in which he specialized in playing brutal and often sadistic thugs. He owned an art gallery on Rodeo Drive during the 1950s. He was an accomplished chef who enjoyed hosting intimate dinner parties for his close circle of friends. His most peaceful passion was cultivating orchids, a species of which he named after his *Perry Mason* co-star Barbara Hale.

Perhaps the finest tribute that can be accorded Raymond Burr was when he, Michael J. Fox and Jim Carrey were named the top Canadians in U.S. television in a June 2002 list compiled by the Banff Television Festival.

His passing was noted at the Pasadena Playhouse, where he had studied, with a memorial service on October 1, 1993. During the ceremony, a director's chair bearing his name was placed centre stage while friends paid tribute.

Questions remain about Raymond Burr's personal life. Indeed, he did share a long-time companionship with former actor Robert Benevides, and left his $32 million estate solely to him. But he never exploited the relationship and thus left this world with the decency, grace and humbleness that symbolized his time upon it.

CHAPTER EIGHT

Christopher Plummer
(1929–)

FOR AN ACTOR WITH A STAGE AND FILM BACKGROUND AS extensive and distinguished as that of Christopher Plummer, it is amazing that his reputation is not more widely appreciated by the ticket-buying public. This criticism extends even to his birth country of Canada, where he is respected, if not revered, by the arts community, but has a relatively low identification factor among contemporary audiences. Certainly his face is recognizable, though people may be hard pressed to place his name. His talents have enhanced many a motion picture, yet his billing alone is unlikely to draw patrons into movie theatres, unlike Arnold Schwarzenegger or Bruce Willis. Possibly that is exactly the career path that Christopher has chosen to follow. This distinguished thespian has never sought celebrity or superstar status, instead choosing to work at and continually improve upon his craft.

And by doing so, Christopher Plummer has excelled in all performing mediums, even while battling personal difficulties including a severe drinking problem that for a performer less

disciplined and dedicated could have had tragic career consequences.

Fortunately, Christopher overcame his alcohol addiction and continues to accumulate an impressive array of credits that have earned him the status of a true acting legend, and he has received many honours and awards in recognition of his achievements, including being invested as a Companion of the Order of Canada.

Arthur Christopher Orme Plummer was born in Toronto, Ontario, on Friday, December 13, 1929, not long after the infamous "Black Tuesday," which was better known as the Great Stock Market Crash of October 24. His father, John Plummer, held a position as secretary to the dean of science at Montréal's McGill University. Christopher's mother, Isabella Mary Plummer, had family ties to the country's political establishment. Her grandfather, John Abbott, had been the former mayor of Montréal and later achieved the post of third prime minister of Canada.

Sadly, by the time of Christopher's birth, his parents were undergoing a separation that would lead to a divorce. Isabella took the baby and moved to Montréal. Despite the nationwide economic collapse, those first years were not particularly difficult for mother and child to endure. Christopher attended Jennings Rice, a fine private school, and was further "tutored" by educated and well-read aunts who were eager to impart their own knowledge to their impressionable young nephew.

Young Christopher's interest in the arts was inspired by the discovery that he was related to playwright Guy du Maurier and the wonderful character actor Nigel Bruce. Bruce, despite roles in dozens of films, would always be best remembered as the doddering Dr. Watson, playing second fiddle to Basil Rathbone's Sherlock Holmes in a popular series of films during the 1940s. Isabella encouraged and further nurtured her son's artistic interests by exposing him to such cultural concepts as the ballet, opera and theatre.

Christopher absorbed each of these new creative endeavours with apparent enthusiasm, but it was not until he worked as a lighting designer for a high school production of *A Midsummer Night's Dream* that he seriously considered a career on the stage. By the time he was in his mid-teens, he'd landed leading roles in school productions. He later recalled his role as D'Arcy in *Pride and Prejudice* as the first wonderful part he ever had the opportunity to play. At age 17, he played his first Shakespearean role, Posthumus in *Cymbeline*, which was directed by Fyodor Komisarjevsky of Moscow's Imperial Theatre and the Old Vic.

Foregoing college, Christopher instead took his post-graduate training with the Canadian Repertory Company in Ottawa where, in just three short years, his talents landed him 75 different roles.

Christopher's acting talent was obviously a gift, and he quickly benefited from it. His first paying job was in a production of *The Infernal Machine*, which, besides providing a welcome salary, also gave Christopher the opportunity to work alongside fellow Montréal native William Shatner. Christopher's talents were soon recognized by the CBC, who hired him for a series of radio dramas, then quickly moved him into their new medium of television, where he was seen in many Canadian-produced dramas, most notably *Othello* (1951).

Christopher was soon taken aboard by the Bermuda Repertory Theatre as one of the company's top players. He quickly added impressive stage credentials to his resumé, including the roles of Ben in *The Little Foxes* and Bernard Kersal in *The Constant Wife*, but most particularly and unusually, the part of killer-on-the-loose Duke Mantee in *The Petrified Forest*, the role that established Humphrey Bogart as a star.

Perhaps Christopher's greatest coup came when he was asked by veteran actor Edward Everett Horton to play the role originated by David Niven in the U.S. tour of *Nina*. The 24-year-old Christopher was delighted and delivered such a fine performance that, within a year, he was appearing in his first Broadway role as George Phillips in *The Starcross Story* (1954). Unfortunately, this was not an auspicious New York debut, as the play closed after just one performance. Still, Christopher made enough of an impression on both critics and audiences that he was next awarded a part opposite Katherine Cornell and Tyrone Power in *The Dark is Light*, followed by the role of gangster Manchester Monaghan in *Home is the Hero*, another short-lived Broadway offering. But he remained passionate about Shakespeare and relished the opportunity to play the roles of Marc Anthony in *Julius Caesar* and Ferdinand in *The Tempest*, both in 1955. Yet perhaps his most acclaimed stage performance was as the Earl of Warwick in *The Lark*, in which he acted alongside Julie Harris and Boris Karloff.

The play ran for 229 performances, and it was on the strength of this part that Christopher was signed for his first motion picture, the Sidney Lumet–directed *Stage Struck* (1958), in which Christopher essayed the role of playwright Joe Sheridan. His top-billed co-stars were Henry Fonda and Susan Strasberg, the daughter of legendary acting coach Lee Strasberg. That same year, he also appeared as a Florida game warden in *Wind Across the Everglades*, a forgettable film notable mainly for providing the screen debut of a pre-*Columbo* Peter Falk.

Despite the growing opportunity for film work, Christopher first and foremost maintained an allegiance to the stage and became a leading actor in the Shakespearean Company at the Stratford Festival. In 1956 and 1957, he played in a variety of the Bard's classics, including the title roles in *Hamlet* and *Macbeth*.

Christopher was pleased with his professional success, and his personal life had taken a turn for the better as well. In 1956, he married actress Tammy Grimes. Unfortunately, the marriage did not last, though it produced Christopher's only child, Amanda, who was born on March 23, 1957. Amanda has followed in her father's footsteps and is an award-winning actress. In 1962, Christopher wed again, this time to journalist Patricia Audrey Lewis, whom he divorced in 1967. His third attempt at matrimony, to British actress Elaine Taylor in 1969, has been his most lasting union.

Christopher began to appear regularly on many of the more popular television dramatic series of the day. Continuing his association with the classics, he played *Oedipus Rex* on Omnibus, following that up with the role of Miles Hendon in *The Prince and the Pauper*, broadcast by CBS on October 28, 1957. In 1962, he assumed the title role of *Cyrano de Bergerac* for NBC. But Christopher's proudest moment on television came in 1964, when he was approached by NBC to star in their special broadcast presentation of *Hamlet*, which was produced to honour the 400th birthday of William Shakespeare. Christopher gave a stunning interpretation of the "melancholy Dane" that was acclaimed by critics. The show went on to play in 30 countries.

Because of Christopher's success in the classics, his services were in demand in Hollywood.

In fact, Christopher made such an impression as the villain Commodus in the costume epic *The Fall of the Roman Empire* (1963) that he was immediately sought after to appear in other big-budget pictures. Renowned director Robert Wise cast Christopher in the Rogers and Hammerstein blockbuster *The Sound of Music* (1965). In what is probably his best-remembered film, Christopher played Baron von Trapp, a cold Austrian military captain who is initially supportive of the German cause, but soon comes to realize the truth behind the Nazi agenda. Co-starring Julie Andrews as Maria, the movie was an enormous critical and box office success, though Christopher didn't share the public's enthusiasm, often referring to the picture as "The Sound of Mucus." Despite his personal feelings, *The Sound of Music* went on to earn $163.2 million and win five Academy Awards, including Best Picture.

Christopher continued to appear in many other important movies. Some of his more memorable titles include *Inside Daisy Clover* (1965), *The Night of the Generals* (1967), in which he played Field Marshall Rommel, Orson Welles' *Oedipus the King* (1968), playing the title role, *Battle of Britain* (1969), *Waterloo* (1970), in which he took on the role of the Duke of Wellington to Rod Steiger's Napoleon and *The Man Who Would Be King* (1975), as Rudyard Kipling. One of his most popular roles was that of famed sleuth Sherlock Holmes, on the trail of Jack the Ripper, in *Murder by Decree* (1979), co-starring James Mason as Dr. Watson.

Other screen triumphs include supporting parts in *Malcolm X* (1992), *The Insider* (1999), in which he gave a brilliant performance as *60 Minutes* reporter Mike Wallace, *A Beautiful Mind* (2001) and more recently *Alexander* (2004), as Aristotle.

While Christopher usually based his film choices more on artistic preference than commercial potential, he was certainly not averse to accepting roles that had both. Perhaps, ironically because of feature-hiding makeup, his most "visible" role to the popcorn-buying public was as the evil Klingon General Chang in *Star Trek VI: The Undiscovered Country* (1991), where he played opposite fellow Canadian and long-ago stage co-player William Shatner.

On television, he appeared in the acclaimed miniseries *Jesus of Nazareth* (1977), as the wicked Herod Antipas, *The Thorn Birds* (1983) and *The Scarlet and the Black* (1983). In 1976, he won a well-deserved Emmy for his role as Roscoe Heyward in *Arthur Hailey's The Moneychangers* (1976).

Christopher also holds the distinction of being the only Canadian actor to play both a Canadian prime minister, John A. Macdonald in the 1979 CBC miniseries *Riel*, and a U.S. president, Franklin Delano Roosevelt in *Winchell* (1998).

Despite these distinguished credentials, it is inevitable that with over 130 motion pictures to his credit, Christopher has also made his share of flops. Perhaps the nadir of his career was *The Clown at Midnight* (1998), a boring direct-to-video horror flick filmed in Winnipeg, where, at the predictable climax, Christopher's character, the mysterious Mr. Caruthers, is revealed to be the title villain.

Incredibly, given his enormous productivity, Christopher drank heavily. Perhaps his drinking never interfered with his work, as he continued to deliver stunning performances both on stage and screen, but it obviously was a major factor in the breakup of his first two marriages.

Christopher was aware that his drinking was out of control, as it was with one of Christopher's idols, the talented yet tragic John Barrymore. Barrymore eventually self-destructed, and that might have been Christopher's course as well but for the love and support of third wife Elaine. He'd met actress Elaine Taylor on the set of *Lock Up Your Daughters* (1969), and she helped Christopher finally overcome his demon. As he said: "She was intelligent enough to realize she had married a wreck, and she did something about it and nursed me back to life again." In an odd twist of fate, in 1997, Christopher played John Barrymore on Broadway in a one-man show that earned the actor a Tony, among other awards. The *New York Times,* in its review of the production, hailed Christopher as "the finest classical actor in North America."

Today, Christopher and Elaine live a comfortable and quiet life on a 30-acre estate just north of New York City. They share a mutual passion for renovating old homes, with Christopher managing the architectural details and Elaine the interior decorating. He still maintains a busy work schedule, though, with his acting services in demand all over the world. Despite his home in the U.S. and his worldwide travels, Christopher Plummer still remains a proud Canadian.

CHAPTER NINE

Gordon Pinsent
(1930–)

IT MAY BE ARGUED THAT OF ALL THE ACTORS PROFILED IN THIS book, Gordon Pinsent is the least recognized. As with Christopher Plummer, his face is familiar, but his name may not instantly register. However, his talents and pride in his Canadian heritage are respected and have been acknowledged with numerous awards and accolades. Gordon has chosen to retain Canada as his home ground and has indeed performed a major part of his work in his native country. Arguably, this is most likely the reason he lacks the international movie identification enjoyed by expatriate Canadian celebrities such as Lorne Greene, Raymond Burr, Christopher Plummer and Donald Sutherland. In addition, for the most part, Gordon has chosen to act in quiet, more intimate pictures that he finds personally pleasing, rather than appearing in megabuck Hollywood blockbusters filled with car crashes and explosions. Yet despite his preferences, Gordon Pinsent retains a reputation as one of the industry's busiest actors, consistently displaying that standard most appreciated by the entertainment community: versatility.

He possesses no snobbery when it comes to the areas of the business in which he chooses to work. Although Gordon has amassed an impressive film resumé, he is probably better known for his television appearances, most of which have been in Canadian productions. In this medium, he has worked as actor, director, producer and writer, and in each capacity has turned out a body of quality entertainment. But Gordon's creative energies don't stop there. He has written six novels and has even penned his autobiography, *By the Way*, which was published to positive reviews in 1992.

Despite his busy work schedule, Gordon has many hobbies, including painting, hiking and swimming. He is also a man who believes in sharing the good fortune he has enjoyed. To that end, he is active in charitable works for Toronto's Hospital for Sick Children and the Easter Seals Telethon, which he hosted in 1998.

Gordon has no plans to retire, but should he eventually make that decision, his acting legacy will live on. The Pinsent talent gene has obviously been passed on to Gordon's children. Daughter Leah, from his second marriage to Charmion King, is an accomplished actress who, in fact, has acted with her father, and son Barry Kennedy, from Gordon's first marriage, is both an actor and an author.

Gordon Edward Pinsent was born in Grand Falls, Newfoundland, on July 12, 1930. He was one of six children born to Stephen Arthur and Flossie Pinsent, along with brothers Harry and Haig and sisters Nita, Hazel and Lil (who passed away in 1998).

As a child, Gordon was known by the unflattering nickname of "Porky," but from as far back as he can remember, he dreamed of performing. Eager to pursue this ambition, he left home at 17 and travelled west to Winnipeg. Gordon may have possessed enthusiasm, but he lacked experience, and to survive, he took a job as an instructor at the Arthur Murray Dance Academy. At the same time, he supplemented his income and fulfilled some of his artistic passion by working as a commercial artist and portrait painter.

He also served with the Royal Canadian Regiment from 1948 to 1951. After leaving the military, he married his first wife, Irene Reid. They had two children, Barry and Beverly, and divorced in 1956.

One night, after attending a play at the Winnipeg Repertory Theatre, Gordon had the chance to speak with theatre owner Leena Lovegrove about possibly performing in one of the company's plays. Leena invited Pinsent to read for the role of a doctor, a small part that would afford him only four lines. Instead of jumping at the opportunity, the budding thespian stretched the truth by replying that he had never played small parts, only leads. Amazingly, his brashness worked, and he was given the lead role.

Gordon was obviously impressive in his theatre debut, as he was next given the role of Sebastian in his first Shakespearean venture, *Twelfth Night*. He quickly established his reputation on the stage and remained with the Winnipeg Repertory Company from 1954 to 1960. Gordon later played at the Manitoba Theatre Centre, performing such roles as George in John Steinbeck's *Of Mice and Men*, Johnny Pope in *A Hatful of Rain* and even took a turn at screwball comedy as the hapless Mortimer Brewster in *Arsenic and Old Lace*. He also held the distinction of performing in the first live radio drama out of Winnipeg.

Hoping to expand his horizons, Gordon headed east, where he performed at Ontario's Stratford Festival. Although Gordon loved the stage, he was not opposed to performing on television. He was offered a part on the series *The Last of the Mohicans*, where another aspect of his character was revealed. The role required that he know how to ride a horse—a skill Gordon had never acquired. Yet when the director asked him if he could ride, the actor replied: "Western or English?" Gordon won the role, but it didn't take the director long to see that he was not the expert he claimed to be.

In 1962, Gordon married his current wife, Charmion King, with whom he had daughter Leah. Charmion is recognized as one of the grand ladies of the Canadian theatre scene and has long been associated with the Stratford Festival. She was born in 1925, making her five years older than

Gordon. Although most recognized for her stage work, she also has appeared in several films and made-for-TV dramas such as *Anne of Green Gables* (1985), in which she played Aunt Josephine. She also played opposite her husband, Gordon, in *Who Has Seen the Wind* (1977), essaying the role of Miss Abercrombie.

Also in 1962, Gordon starred in his second TV series, *Scarlett Hill*, which ran from 1962 through 1964. A more popular show in which he appeared was *The Forest Rangers* (1963–66), playing the square-jawed Sergeant Scott.

Gordon was in demand as an actor and began appearing regularly on television, showing up in guest starring roles on both sides of the border on such popular programs as *It Takes a Thief, Marcus Welby, M.D., Cannon* and *Banacek.* On Canadian television, he was seen in *Adventures in Rainbow Country, Street Legal, Lonesome Dove: The Series* and *Road to Avonlea,* among many others. He even played the title role on the Canadian-produced *Quentin Durgens, M.P.* (1966–71).

For a time during the late 1960s, with so much American television work coming his way, Gordon moved his family to California. He recalls becoming friendly with the legendary Marlon Brando and attended a drive-in movie with Brando's wife and children.

Besides his work on U.S. television, Gordon suddenly found himself in demand for movie roles.

He made his American debut opposite Steve McQueen and Faye Dunaway in the caper classic *The Thomas Crown Affair* (1968), directed by Canadian Norman Jewison. Although he was billed down the cast list, Gordon made a major leap forward (both in billing and role) in his next picture *Colossus: The Forbin Project* (1970). Third-billed Gordon plays The President in this science-fiction suspense thriller about a super-intelligent computer that turns against humans. As reviewed in *Leonard Maltin's Movie Guide*, the film is "chilling and believable." Gordon himself received good reviews for playing his part with "concern and conviction."

Gordon returned to the chiller genre in 1972 when he took on the role of Lt. Jack Peters, a 1970s Los Angeles detective on the trail of Blacula in the film of the same name. The film was a fun fright flick and received generally good notices. But most of the reviews went to Shakespearean actor William Marshall, who played the title character, with Gordon almost being lost in the shuffle.

This may have proven upsetting to Gordon, for that same year saw the release of *The Rowdyman*, based on his acclaimed novel. Gordon both wrote the screenplay and starred as Jack Cole, a rather shiftless man who accidentally causes the death of a childhood friend. The beautifully filmed movie was made entirely in Newfoundland and earned Gordon critical plaudits both for his script and acting.

Gordon moved back to Canada, where he began getting parts in films of beauty and/or substance, such as the TV movie *Who Has Seen the Wind* (1977), based on the W.O. Mitchell book about growing up in Saskatchewan during the Depression. He then played Ambassador Ken Taylor in *Escape from Iran: The Canadian Caper* (1981), the harrowing true story of the Canadian Embassy's attempt to rescue American diplomats during the Iranian Revolution.

Gordon's next movie saw him in the true-life story of Olive Frederickson, *Silence of the North* (1981). Ellen Burstyn played Olive, whose independence grows from her need to survive in the winter wilderness after her first husband is presumably killed while trapping for food. Gordon gives both a strong and sensitive performance as John Frederickson, a bush pilot who becomes her second husband.

In 1987, another of Gordon's novels was brought to the screen. This time he not only starred and scripted, but also directed the picture. *John and the Missus* is the touching story of what happens to a small Newfoundland community when its sole source of income—a local mine—is closed down. Gordon gives a strong performance as John Munn, the one man who refuses to accept the pittance the government offers following the mine closure, thus incurring the wrath of his fellow townspeople. As with *The Rowdyman*, *John and the Missus* was adapted into a stage play, with

Gordon playing the lead role at the Neptune Theatre premiere in Halifax.

Up to this point, Gordon Pinsent had never been
regarded as a comic actor. But that changed when
he took on the role of habitual liar Hap Shaughnessy on the CBC comedy *The Red Green Show*
(1991). At the time, the program was undergoing
a ratings slump, and series star and creator Steve
Smith thought that by introducing this new character, the ratings might improve. His friend Gordon
offered to work for scale, but ended up creating a
character that became instantly popular with
viewers, putting the show back on track.

Even though he admitted that Hap Shaughnessy
was "not an easy man to play," Gordon thoroughly
enjoyed the experience and continued making
comedic inroads with a recurring role on CTV's
popular series *Due South* (1994–98).

On the show, he played Robert Fraser, the father
of lead character Benton Fraser (Paul Gross) and...
a dead man. For the pilot episode, Gordon merely
provided the dead character's voice, prompting
Gordon to remark: "You can phone them in, be
obscenely paid and just go into a voice."

But when the pilot was picked up for a series,
his supernatural character was given form by producer Paul Haggis. Robert Fraser's "ghost," attired
in a Mountie uniform, provided his son with coun-
sel, but usually at the most inopportune moments.

There seems to be no end to Gordon Pinsent's talents. Nor is there any dearth of work. He's gone from providing the voice of King Babar in both the motion picture *Babar: The Movie* (1989) and subsequent animated series, to a strong supporting role as the Newfoundland newspaperman in the critically acclaimed *The Shipping News* (2001), in which he provided the model for the Newfoundland accent for the rest of the cast.

Newfoundland remains important to Gordon. He set his 1997 play *Corner Green* in his hometown of Grand Falls, a community of just 15,000. The province also figured prominently in *Win, Again!* (2000), a powerful CBC telefilm written by and starring Gordon as a man who returns to his wife and son after being on the run for 14 years for a murder he didn't commit. His daughter Leah also appears in the movie as the girlfriend of his estranged son.

Along the way, Gordon has racked up a whole array of awards, for both his acting and writing, including an Actra Award for his 1971 Christmas movie *A Gift to Last*, two Gemini Awards in 1999 for his screenplay *Win, Again!* and Best Supporting Actor for his role of Duff McArdle, owner of the team in the hockey series *Power Play* (1998–2000). Previously, he had won Geminis for his guest appearance on the courtroom series *Street Legal* and for his work on *Due South*. Among other honours Gordon has amassed, he has received three lifetime achievement awards, including the John

Drainie and Earl Grey Awards for his body of work as an actor and for his significant contribution to television. In June 2004, he was presented with the Banff TV Festival's Award of Excellence. He holds three honorary doctorates and received an LLD (Doctor of Laws) from the University of Prince Edward Island. In 1980, he was made an Officer of the Order of Canada.

CHAPTER TEN

Donald Sutherland
(1934–)

THROUGHOUT HIS INTERNATIONAL MOTION PICTURE CAREER, which spans 40-plus years, Donald Sutherland has maintained strong ties to his country of origin. He has remained true to his Canadian roots, and Canada has reciprocated by awarding him with the Order of Canada for his many outstanding film roles and his generous contribution to the national cinema scene.

Donald Sutherland has never been an easy actor to categorize. He has deliberately never allowed himself to be defined by one kind of role. Unlike Lorne Greene, Raymond Burr and William Shatner, each of whom, despite their individual versatility, became firmly identified with a singular character, Donald has skirted the field. From playing a not-too-bright prisoner of war given the opportunity to redeem himself on a World War II suicide mission to a private eye searching for a missing husband to a husband and father coming to grips with the death of a child, this talented actor has refused to be pigeonholed.

His film preferences have truly been eclectic, much as the man himself. Donald Sutherland

became a movie star despite not having conventional leading man looks. He is 6'4" tall and lanky, with an almost cadaverous face and a monotonous voice better suited to Roger Corman projects than films directed by Robert Aldrich or Robert Redford. But Donald has become one of the most bankable actors in the industry, perhaps because there is no snobbery about him. He will as quickly embrace a direct-to-video release (provided the role offers sufficient challenge) as he will a multimillion-dollar screen blockbuster. Of course at age 71, Donald has settled into character roles. But there is no question that, regardless of the size of the part, his presence continues to enhance the entertainment value of any project he undertakes. It certainly says much about the talent of the actor that his accomplishments have not been overshadowed by the success of his most famous offspring, son Kiefer.

Donald McNichol Sutherland hails from Saint John, New Brunswick, where he was born July 17, 1934. He grew up in Bridgewater, where he suffered from polio in childhood. He recovered and soon after developed an interest in the entertainment industry. By the time he was 14, he was already a radio DJ.

Despite this early success in broadcasting, when Donald graduated from high school, he enrolled at the University of Toronto as an engineering student. However, it didn't take him long to discover his true passion for acting, and upon graduating, he decided to pursue his theatrical ambitions. His intentions may have been dedicated, but he quickly discovered that opportunities were scarce. His hope to enroll at the London Academy of Music and Dramatic Arts came to naught—not because Donald lacked talent, but because his height and rather offbeat appearance did not fit in with the British perception of how a leading man should look. Donald was undaunted and promptly offered his services to a British repertory theatre, which appreciated the young actor's talents and cast him in a variety of stage roles.

By now Donald was married to his first wife Lois Hardwick. They had wed in 1959, and it would be a seven-year union, lasting until 1966.

Soon Donald began receiving film offers. His first movie role came in 1963, in a forgotten picture called *The World Ten Times Over*, in which he was billed as "the man in the nightclub." Appropriately, given his gaunt, mildly sinister appearance, he was cast opposite genre icon Christopher Lee in the Italian horror picture *Il Castello dei morti vivi* (*Castle of the Living Dead*). In this 1964 film, movie neophyte Donald was afforded *three* roles: as a young soldier, an old man and a witch! While hardly an auspicious beginning for a burgeoning performer, Donald did manage to attract the attention of the producers of *The Bedford Incident* (1965), who cast him in the small role of Hospitalman Nerny in this

Cold War thriller starring Richard Widmark and Sidney Poitier.

Then it was back to horror as Donald appeared in the final episode of the Amicus Pictures production, *Dr. Terror's House of Horrors* (1965). In this intelligently plotted thriller, which reunited Donald with Christopher Lee, Donald played one of five men huddled together in a train compartment who has his future foretold by the mysterious Dr. Schreck (Peter Cushing). In Donald's story, his character, Dr. Bob Carroll, has the misfortune of being married to a vampire. He is told how to dispose of his blood-seeking bride by a senior medical colleague (portrayed by Max Adrian), but the episode ends with a twist.

Donald's third horror film offering was *Die! Die! My Darling!* (1965) In this outing, which co-starred an aging Tallulah Bankhead and an up-and-coming Stefanie Powers, Donald played the role of Joseph, a mentally impaired handyman. Once more, Donald's participation in the project was little more than "window dressing."

It is probable that Donald's career may not have progressed much further if not for director Robert Aldrich, who again capitalized on Donald's unique looks and demeanour, casting him as Vernon L. Pinkley in the classic World War II film *The Dirty Dozen* (1967). Once again, Donald was cast as a mentally impaired character—and homicidal to boot—but his role was given dimension, and he

was given several key scenes in which his character was allowed to shine. This was no small accom-
plishment given that virtual screen newcomer
Donald was sharing acting time with such veterans
as Lee Marvin, Ernest Borgnine and Charles Bron-
son. Pinkley is one of the "dozen" who does not
survive to the closing credits, but Donald Sutherland the actor was about to embark on an incredible cinematic journey.

In another kind of journey, Donald married
Shirley Douglas, daughter of Canadian New
Democratic Party leader Tommy Douglas, in 1966.
Although the marriage was a short one, ending in
1970, it produced twins Rachel and Kiefer (named
after producer Warren Kiefer, who had given Donald
his first film break by casting him in an Italian horror thriller). Kiefer, after a rough period involving
alcoholism and other personal difficulties, has gone
on to have a substantial acting career of his own.

Donald's next series of films cast him in supporting roles, including the 1968 heist movie *The Split*, in
which he was part of a strong co-starring team that
consisted of his *Dirty Dozen* co-player Ernest Borgnine, along with Gene Hackman, Warren Oates and
James Whitmore. Despite this powerhouse cast, the
movie proved to be a dismal failure.

However, in 1970, Donald really came into his
own when he assumed the role of Dr. Benjamin
Franklin "Hawkeye" Pierce in Robert Altman's
movie version of *M*A*S*H*. This irreverent look at

life in a medical unit during the Korean War was a critical and commercial box office S*M*A*S*H. Donald achieved instant stardom.

Donald used his sudden celebrity to speak out against the Vietnam War with his then romantic partner and vocal protestor Jane Fonda. Donald's anti-war stance endeared him to young people opposed to the conflict, but it created some tense moments with the Hollywood establishment, into whose ranks Donald had recently entered.

Fortunately, his popularity was on the upswing. After playing a leading role in *Start the Revolution Without Me* (1970), in which Donald co-starred with Gene Wilder and Orson Welles, he appeared opposite paramour Jane Fonda in the Alan J. Pakula–directed mystery *Klute* (1971), playing the title role of the private eye on the case, John Klute.

Donald's subsequent film choices were eclectic to say the least. He had achieved leading-man status, but stardom was apparently not his due. He chose the starring part of a film director in Paul Mazursky's self-indulgent *Alex in Wonderland* (1970), which featured a strong supporting cast that included Ellen Burstyn, Jeanne Moreau and even famed director Frederico Fellini.

Donald continued to appear in films with little commercial value, but which had personal meaning, such as another anti-establishment flick co-starring Jane Fonda, *F.T.A.* (1972), which was really a documentary of Donald and Fonda's anti-war skits presented at army bases.

In 1972, Donald married Francine Racette, a union that has endured. The marriage has produced three sons: Roeg, born in 1974 and named after Donald's *Don't Look Now* director, Nicholas Roeg; Rossif, born in 1978; and Angus Redford, born in 1979 and named for another Sutherland director, Robert Redford, who helmed *Ordinary People*.

Donald's film career continued as he appeared opposite Julie Christie in Nicholas Roeg's supernatural thriller *Don't Look Now* (1973). In this underrated suspense classic, Donald plays John Baxter, the father of a drowned child whose spirit torments its parents throughout a trip to Venice.

In an attempt to reprise their earlier success, Donald joined *M*A*S*H* co-star Elliott Gould in *S*P*Y*S* (1974), an 84-minute time-waster directed by Irvin Kershner that didn't significantly advance Donald's career.

However, the following year, Donald made a cinematic impact in John Schlessinger's *The Day of the Locust*. In this disturbing film based on Nathaneal West's novel about the desperate lives of Hollywood "fringies," Donald's character is particularly despicable as he tramples a young girl to death before being torn apart by a vengeful crowd at a 1930s Hollywood premiere. While Donald is top-billed in the picture, his character does not make his entrance until 42 minutes into the film.

Donald's identification with international film properties continued when he was cast as the lead in *Fellini's Casanova* (1976). Although an opulent production, the movie, filmed entirely at Rome's Cinecitta Studios, did not attract a wide audience. Nor did the five-and-a-half-hour *1900*, directed by Bernardo Bertolucci.

The actor returned to mainstream success when he appeared as the pot-smoking college professor in *National Lampoon's Animal House* (1978). Donald and fellow Canadian John Vernon are billed down the cast list, their roles overshadowed by the mugging of John Belushi, but Donald still managed to make an impression among youth audiences with his metaphysics-expounding Professor Dave Jennings.

Another of Donald's commercial projects was the remake of *Invasion of the Body Snatchers* (1978). In the picture, Donald played health inspector Matthew Bennell, the first to conceive of the alien conspiracy and one of the last to become "replaced" by its malevolent life spore. He followed that up with supporting roles in *Murder by Decree* (1979), as a Jack the Ripper suspect, and *The Great Train Robbery* (1979), co-starring with Sean Connery in a picture based on true events and directed by author Michael Crichton.

Donald received his highest professional accolades to date when he appeared as Calvin Jarrett in Robert Redford's directorial debut *Ordinary People* (1980).

The picture, based on Judith Guest's novel about a well-to-do family trying to cope with the death of their eldest son, won Redford a Best Director Academy Award, along with a Best Supporting Actor Award for co-star Timothy Hutton (who, sadly, has not gone on to better things). Donald and co-star Mary Tyler Moore were overlooked in the awards category, but both delivered strong performances in this unforgettable film.

Donald maintained his career momentum by next starring opposite fellow Canadian Kate Nelligan in

the film adaptation of Ken Follett's bestselling novel *Eye of the Needle* (1981). Donald played the Nazi villain Faber, who insinuates himself into the life of the widowed and sexually frustrated Lucy (Nelligan). At the film's climax, Lucy dispatches her tormentor with a well-placed rock.

His next major film role saw Donald as Sergeant Major Peasy in the mega-bomb *Revolution* (1985). Although populated with a strong cast consisting of (a miscast) Al Pacino, Nastassja Kinski, Graham Greene and Robbie Coltrane, this picture proved to be an ill-conceived venture that failed to catch on with audiences and critics.

Donald didn't fare any better in his leading role as South African schoolteacher Ben du Toit in the apartheid drama *A Dry White Season* (1989). Despite a co-starring appearance by Marlon Brando, this potentially powerful film missed the mark with its hollow and contrived presentation.

Where Donald established his most recognized character was with his powerful and moving performance as Dr. Norman Bethune in the 1977 TV film *Bethune*. He played the controversial Canadian doctor who aided Mao Tse-tung's army during its famous march. Donald made the part his own, and he later reprised the role in the 1990 theatrical release *Bethune: The Making of a Hero*. While the latter film was allotted a more substantial budget, it was the earlier production that most agree stands as the definitive version of Bethune's life.

Donald's starring films, however, were not breaking box office records. He was achieving more success in supporting roles, such as the arsonist Ronald Bartel in Ron Howard's *Backdraft* (1991). Donald is genuinely chilling as the psychopathic firebug about to be released on parole, whose defence is crushed by fire investigator Robert De Niro. He had another strong if brief appearance as the informant "X," who cited the assassination conspiracy in Oliver Stone's *JFK* (1991).

Perhaps Donald's most commercially popular role was as Merrick Jamison-Smythe, the tutor of the lead character in *Buffy the Vampire Slayer* (1992). This was a part that initially embarrassed Donald, as friends could not understand how an actor of his stature could appear in a picture with such a title. However, Donald creates a most credible character given the absurd dimensions of the plot—and provides a most poignant death scene, while handing the mantle of "slayer" or "the chosen one" to the teenage Valley Girl Buffy (Kristy Swanson).

Six Degrees of Separation followed in 1993. Again Donald played a supporting part, secondary to Will Smith, in a film that scored better in video outlets than it did in theatrical release.

Donald finally received industry recognition for his talents as Colonel Mikhail Fetisov in the made-for-television chiller *Citizen X* (1995), the true story of serial killer Andrei Chikatilo. For his role, Donald was awarded both an Emmy and a Golden Globe.

In *A Time to Kill* (1996), Donald had the opportunity to act with son Kiefer in the film adaptation of John Grisham's bestselling novel. He also gave excellent support as track coach Bill Bowerman in Robert Towne's *Without Limits* (1998), the true story of the late University of Oregon runner and Munich Olympic participant Steve Prefontaine.

Donald maintains a busy schedule, performing both in theatrical presentations and direct-to-video releases. He remains one of the industry's most versatile actors and is effective both as an offbeat hero or a slimy, despicable villain. Recent film roles have showcased Donald in both categories. In *Space Cowboys* (2000), as engineer Jerry O'Neill, Donald is part of a senior troupe (including Clint Eastwood, Tommy Lee Jones and James Garner), sent into the cosmos to correct a problem with an obsolete Russian satellite that only they have the technological knowledge to comprehend. The picture, also directed by Eastwood, was a welcome popular success for Donald, grossing nearly $129 million worldwide.

In *The Italian Job* (2003), Donald received third billing for his role as master thief John Bridger. The picture was a caper movie with the usual betrayal aspect. In this case, his character is murdered by Edward Norton, precipitating revenge by daughter Stella (Charlize Theron in an early role), who organizes the gang to get even with the duplicitous Norton. It seemed as if Donald had hit upon a winning character type that he carried on into his next project.

A British-Romanian-Italian-American film, *Cold Mountain* (2003), based on the bestselling book by Charles Frazier, also served Donald well, though his role was brief. As with many of Donald Sutherland's latter-day characterizations, his part, though small, is significant and helps propel the story forward. His Reverend Monroe proves indispensable to the story line, but expires well before the movie kicks into gear. *Cold Mountain*, which stars Jude Law and Nicole Kidman, served primarily as a showcase for Renée Zellweger, who walked off with a Best Supporting Actress Oscar for her role as the tough-minded character of Ruby Thewes.

Donald truly excels as a movie villain and his part as Richard Straker in the second TV miniseries based on the Stephen King vampire novel *Salem's Lot* (2004) truly stands as testament to his ability to project a frightening menace. As the servant of transplanted vampire Kurt Barlow (Rutger Hauer), Straker is even more ghoulish than his master, assisting in setting up the horrendous nocturnal events that gradually "depopulate" a remote Maine community.

Donald maintained his association with TV horror when that same year he assumed the role of Captain Walton in the umpteenth remake of Mary Shelley's *Frankenstein*. With audiences being bombarded by this oft-told tale, the 2004 version arrived and left network broadcasting with little fanfare.

However, in an upcoming feature film scheduled for 2006, he combines the straight and the horrific in a genuinely eerie horror piece, *An American Haunting*, based on a true-life occurrence. The picture is based on the Bell family witch-hauntings, which are validated by the State of Tennessee as the only case in U.S. history in which an entity may have been responsible for the death—or murder—of a man. More than 20 books have been written on the subject, and the town still lives in fear of the return of the vengeful spirit. In this movie, Donald portrays John Bell, the family patriarch whose character provides the impetus for these supernatural occurrences.

Fortunately, many more movie roles lie on the horizon for Donald Sutherland. Despite his occasional questionable choice of properties, he is a gifted actor whose services remain in demand. His 2005 projects include *Pride and Prejudice*, *American Gun*, *Land of the Blind* and *The Four Saints*.

Although Donald has never really been recognized as a leading man, he remains one of the most reliable actors in the industry. He is hard working and recognizable, and his performances, regardless of their brevity, continue to provide audiences with solid entertainment value as he maintains an ongoing dedication to his craft.

CHAPTER ELEVEN

William Shatner
(1931–)

WILLIAM SHATNER HAS BECOME SO IDENTIFIED WITH THE ROLE of Captain James T. Kirk, commander of the starship *Enterprise*, that many of his other accomplishments have been overlooked. Shatner, a classically trained actor, began performing in Shakespearean roles in his native Canada. He then moved on to Broadway, where he established a reputation as a serious stage actor. Hollywood soon beckoned, where, following a memorable film debut in *The Brothers Karamazov* (1958), he became a fixture in the golden age of television, appearing in episodes of some of the best dramatic programs of the day.

Yet it seems that once Bill entered series television with his classic role as the heroic James T. Kirk in *Star Trek,* his career hit a high and then suffered a creative stall from which it took years to recover. He became so identified with the part that after the series was cancelled, he found himself virtually unemployable, with the exception of supporting parts in made-for-television movies and B pictures. William's fortunes once again soared when Captain Kirk, along with the original crew of the *Enterprise*,

was resurrected for *Star Trek: The Motion Picture* (1979) and its succession of sequels. Fortunately, this talented actor remains in the groove with roles in motion pictures, and he is currently once again enjoying success on the small screen both with the acclaimed series *Boston Legal* and as a well-recognized and highly paid ad pitchman, representing products ranging from bran cereal to Priceline.com.

William Shatner was born in Montréal, Québec, on March 22, 1933, the son of Ann and Joseph Shatner, a garment manufacturer who hoped that his son would follow him into his trade. William attended Verdun High School and later McGill University, seeking a degree in commerce. However, he soon became interested in drama and switched his major to theatre, earning a BA in 1952. During his summers while in college, he performed with the Royal Mount Theatre Company.

Upon graduation, William moved to Ottawa where he joined the National Repertory Theatre, sharing a friendship and professional acquaintance with the likewise up-and-coming Christopher Plummer, for whom he would later understudy in a production of *Henry V.* William received a small salary of $30 a week for his work with the company, which included starring roles in such classical productions as *The Merchant of Venice.* He was also presented with the company's Most Promising

Actor Award. However, accolades aside, he later acknowledged that he would have been far more financially successful had he followed his father into business. But he remained firm in his commitment and maintained that his lack of funds only made him more determined to succeed as an actor. William was grateful for every opportunity to hone his craft and was especially pleased when he was asked to appear at the Stratford Festival, where he was seen in several Shakespearean productions.

He made his screen debut playing a crook in the forgotten Canadian-made feature *The Butler's Night Off* (1951) and even appeared on the CBC children's show *Howdy Doody* (1954) as Ranger Bob. An interesting side note is that future *Star Trek* co-star James Doohan (Scotty) was originally cast as Timber Tom on the program, but wanted more money than the CBC was willing to pay. He was replaced by actor Peter Mews, who was unable to appear the first week of the show and was temporarily replaced by William Shatner.

William moved to New York in 1956, where, despite his stage successes in Canada, he found it difficult to find acting work. Things got so tough that at one point he seriously considered returning to Montréal and capitulating to his father's wishes. That year he also married Canadian actress Gloria Rand, with whom he had three daughters: Leslie Carol (August 31, 1958), Lisabeth Mary (June 12, 1960) and Melanie Ann (August 1, 1964). The couple honeymooned in Scotland, but for William it was a working vacation because he'd been given a role in the Edinburgh Festival production of *Henry V.*

Fortunately, on his return to the U.S. things started to improve for William, and he began racking up impressive stage and early television credentials. On Broadway, he starred in the two-year run of *The World of Susie Wong*, in which he played Robert Lomax, followed by *A Shot in the Dark* with Julie Harris, *L'Idiote* and *Tamburlaine*. He became an early TV fixture, appearing on many of the most powerful dramatic shows of the day, including *Goodyear Playhouse*, *Circle Theatre*, *Philco Playhouse* and *Studio One*. He was also regularly seen on such series as *The Defenders*, *Alfred Hitchcock Presents*, *Thriller* and, perhaps most famously, *The Twilight Zone*. Audiences fondly remember the episode "Nightmare at 20,000 Feet," written by famed fantasy writer Richard Matheson, in which William played Bob Wilson, a man recovering from a nervous breakdown who, while onboard an airplane flight, is unable to convince anyone that a hideous gremlin is attempting to sabotage the plane.

William was signed to a seven-year contract by 20th Century-Fox, who promptly cast him as Alexei in their big-budget production of Dostoyevsky's *The Brothers Karamazov* (1958). William was part of a high-powered cast that included Yul Brynner, Richard Basehart, Claire Bloom and, as the patriarch, the powerful Method actor Lee L. Cobb.

His next major film role came in 1961, when he portrayed Captain Harrison Byers, the aide to Judge Dan Haywood (Spencer Tracy) in Stanley Kramer's *Judgment at Nuremberg*. Although it was a small role, William worked comfortably with the veteran Tracy and, as with all young actors who played alongside the great man, learned much about the intricacies of film acting.

Perhaps not as powerful as *Nuremberg*, yet intriguing enough on its own merits, was another picture William participated in that year called *The Explosive Generation*. In the film, William's character, progressive high school teacher Peter Gifford, fuels the ire of parents when he attempts to teach sex education to his students. While it is a relic of dated morals today, this fact-based movie caused quite a controversy in its time.

William was also involved in another controversial project, *The Intruder* (1962), the film of which director Roger Corman is most proud and, ironically, the only one of his over 100 movies to lose money. In the picture, William is Adam Cramer, a racist who drifts throughout the South inciting townspeople to riot against court-ordered school integration. It is a role in which William does not invoke audience sympathy, but one of the most powerful performances he has delivered on film.

In 1964, William appeared in the all-star remake of the classic Japanese drama *Rashomon, The Outrage*. But despite a cast that included Paul Newman,

Edward G. Robinson and two of William's *Brothers Karamazov* co-stars, Claire Bloom and Albert Salmi, the pretentious movie proved both a critical and commercial misfire. He fared even less well in the little-seen Esperanto-language horror movie *Incubus*, which he made in 1966.

It appeared that William Shatner's film career had hit a standstill. But fortunately, he was soon to become a household name, with his show business immortality assured.

Actor Jeffrey Hunter had been assigned the role of Captain Christopher Pike in the original *Star Trek* pilot titled *The Cage* (1966). When a second pilot was announced, *Where No Man Has Gone Before*, William had assumed command of the starship *Enterprise*, the character now named Captain James Tiberius Kirk.

When the series was given the green light by CBS, William was beamed aboard as Captain Kirk, ably assisted by an ensemble cast that included Leonard Nimoy as Mr. Spock, DeForest Kelley as Dr. "Bones" McCoy, James Doohan as Scotty, George Takei as Sulu, Walter Koenig as Chekov and Nichelle Nichols as Lieutenant Uhura.

Today, with the immense success of the *Star Trek* franchise, it seems inconceivable to many that the series just scraped through its three-season run, frequently facing the threat of cancellation. It was never high in the ratings, nor did it receive much critical attention. But those who embraced the show did so with a passion. When the cancellation of the series was finally announced, fans sent letters to CBS by the score, demanding that the show not be removed from television. And CBS complied—until 1969.

Following the show's demise, William Shatner descended to the lowest point of his professional and personal life. His wife Gloria left him, and the divorce settlement ruined him financially. He was so destitute that he was forced to live in a trailer while slowly trying to re-establish his career post-Kirk by acting in TV movies. Fortunately, the productions in which he appeared were of high quality. William delivered a particularly strong performance as the prosecutor, Lt. Col. N.P. Chipman, in the PBS production of *The Andersonville Trial* (1970), directed by George C. Scott. His other outstanding television achievements include *Vanished* (1971) and the controversial *Go Ask Alice* (1973).

That same year he provided the voice for his animated likeness in the *Star Trek* cartoon series. His motion picture roles were mainly low-budget offerings, such as *Big Bad Mama* (1974), the dreadful Florida-made *Impulse* (1974) and the horror cult favourites *The Devil's Rain* (1975) and *Kingdom of the Spiders* (1977). Unfortunately, most of these projects did little for William either artistically or financially. He had married again in 1973 to Marcy Lafferty and was trying to find the right work to provide them with a stable income. He attempted another television series, *The Barbary Coast*, which co-starred Dennis Cole, but the program lasted only one season (1975–76).

There had always been a small but steadily growing cult surrounding *Star Trek*, which had gained renewed popularity with its airings in syndication. Finally, in 1979, "Trekkies" rejoiced when Paramount Pictures released the long-anticipated movie adaptation, *Star Trek: The Motion Picture*, directed by Robert Wise and co-scripted by the series creator Gene Roddenberry. The original "bridge" cast was assembled, and while admittedly the film did not live up to audience expectations, it was a box office smash, earning $82.3 million and prompting six more *Star Trek* movies between 1979 and 1991, including William's directorial debut in *Star Trek V: The Final Frontier* (1989). William finally retired the character of Captain James T. Kirk when he was killed in the climactic battle of *Star Trek Generations* (1994), which paved the way for the motion picture entry of Captain Jean-Luc Picard from TV's *Star Trek: The Next Generation* (1987–94).

During this period, William had more work than he could handle. He appeared as Sergeant Thomas Hooker on the popular police drama *T.J. Hooker*, which ran from 1982 to 1986. Then he appeared as host of the reality series *Rescue 911* (1989–96).

He also began a second career as a writer, publishing two non-fiction works, *Star Trek Memories*

(1993) and *Get a Life!* (1999), and penning a series of nine books titled *TekWars*, which were later developed into a short-lived television series (1994–96), with William both helping create the series and playing a role. As if that wasn't enough, he entered the business world as CEO of Core Digital Effects, a Toronto-based firm that handles special effects for various motion pictures, including *Fly Away Home* (1996) starring fellow Canadian Anna Paquin.

William enjoys spoofing his image and has done so successfully in films such as *Airplane II: The Sequel* (1982) and *National Lampoon's Loaded Weapon 1* (1993). In a departure from acting, he briefly managed WWF wrestler Bret Hart in 1993.

Sadly, William has experienced his share of pain in his personal life. His marriage to Marcy Lafferty collapsed in 1994. His subsequent (and apparently troubled) marriage to Nerine Kidd ended when she was discovered drowned in the Shatner swimming pool on August 9, 1999. On the health front, besides problems with his weight, William suffers from tinnitus, a chronic and constant ringing in his ears that he acquired during a special-effects explosion on the *Star Trek* set. It is a condition that he admits once led him to consider suicide.

But in recent years, William has rediscovered personal happiness. On February 13, 2001, he married Elizabeth Anderson Martin, a widowed horse trainer. As William is a horse breeder with a farm in Kentucky, he and Elizabeth shared a common interest that soon led to romance.

One of William's most satisfying accomplishments is his work as producer and host of the Hollywood Horse Show, which he founded in 1990. Through this annual event, over $1.25 million has been raised for various children's charities.

Despite industry jibes aimed at his talents as an actor, William was honoured in 1981 with a star on Hollywood's Walk of Fame. He earned a 1999 Emmy nomination for his comic turn as "the Big Giant Head" on *Third Rock from the Sun* and finally won the award in 2004 for his role as attorney Denny Crane on the legal drama *The Practice*. So popular was William's character that he was brought over to the program's spinoff *Boston Legal*, for which he won a Golden Globe in 2005.

Through the many personal and career highs and lows, William Shatner has proven himself a survivor. No one has to tell him to "Get a life!" He's had one.

CHAPTER TWELVE

Leslie Nielsen
(1926–)

LESLIE NIELSEN IS UNQUESTIONABLY ONE OF THE MOST original talents to come from Canada. Everyone recognizes his handsome, if somewhat uncharacteristic leading-man features, accentuated by a prominently broken nose, and can immediately identify his rich, deep, baritone voice. Most are familiar with him through his off-the-wall characterizations in such films as *Airplane!* (1980) and the *Naked Gun* series. His comedy derives from an effective 30-year character transition from the cynical into the bewildered, coupled with a masterful deadpan delivery. His comic incarnations are sincere and dedicated, but his characters are also decidedly clueless—never quite comprehending the situation at hand. The fun is in watching how this ineptitude still manages to prevail against overpowering odds.

Since 1980, Leslie has specialized in this kind of role both in motion pictures and on television. But prior to that, his on-camera persona was as one of the most intense dramatic actors in the business. He played a variety of serious parts, running the gamut from romantic lead to space hero to western

villain, and he was convincing in all of these roles. He enjoyed a solid career playing it straight. But even though it wasn't utilized onscreen, Leslie always possessed an offbeat sense of humour that the team of Jim Abrahams and David and Jerry Zucker recognized when casting for their disaster spoof *Airplane!*, adding him to their roster of other granite-jawed actors not particularly known for their comedic skills. This belated breakthrough film introduced Leslie to a whole new generation of moviegoers. At an age when many actors would be slowing down, he's having the time of his life, and he hasn't looked back yet.

Perhaps Leslie had no choice but to develop an appreciation for the bizarre. Leslie William Nielsen was born of Danish and Welsh parentage on February 11, 1926, in the isolated community of Tulita (formerly Fort Norman) in the Northwest Territories, where his father, a constable in the Royal Canadian Mounted Police, was posted. It was often a lonely life for Leslie, half-brother Gilbert and older sibling Eric, who endured long, bitterly cold winters and had to find ways to amuse themselves. Leslie would joke that their home was so far north that the famous John Wayne picture about gold prospectors should be retitled *"South" to Alaska*. While Leslie was the family funny man, brother Eric became active in Canadian politics, serving as the Government Leader of the Yukon Territory before becoming a Member of Parliament and the Deputy Prime Minister of Canada.

Their father was a strict disciplinarian, and to avoid punishment for his occasional mischievous behaviour, Leslie concocted elaborate lies. He later said that those untruths were his first introduction to acting. He may also have possessed a genetic predisposition to the profession because his uncle was Jean Hersholt. Hersholt was a strong supporting player in such pictures as the Erich von Stoheim–directed *Greed* (1925) and the Boris Karloff flick *The Mask of Fu Manchu* (1932). Also, the Jean Hersholt Humanitarian Award presented annually at the Academy Award ceremonies is named for him.

The family finally moved to Edmonton, Alberta, when Eric started school. Leslie recalled that he was about four years old at the time. He enjoyed a creative incentive when at age five, he saw his first film, Boris Karloff's *Frankenstein* (1931), which had a great effect on him, and he became fascinated with motion pictures. Leslie then discovered a love of acting through his teacher, a man named Mr. Stockwell, who introduced his young pupil to Shakespeare and cast Leslie as the lead in an elementary school version of *Romeo and Juliet*. Following graduation from Victoria Composite High School, he enlisted in the Royal Canadian Air Force in 1944. He trained as an aerial gunner, but served for only a year before the war ended, never seeing action.

Returning to civilian life, Leslie got a job at a Calgary radio station. His duties included working as an engineer, disc jockey and announcer. Leslie found he enjoyed show business and decided to expand his horizons. He enrolled in Lorne Greene's Academy of Radio Arts, where he first discovered he had a true talent for acting beyond grade school dramatics. He was awarded a scholarship to study at the prestigious Neighborhood Playhouse in New York City. He studied theatre with the renowned drama coach Stanford Meisner, attended the Actor's Studio and even took dance lessons with Martha Graham.

With his training behind him, Leslie put his talents to practical use and performed summer stock. In 1950, he married his second wife, Monica Boyer, whom he divorced in 1956 (apparently he'd been married previously to Barbaree Earl, of whom little is known, though she later appeared in two of his films: *Dracula: Dead and Loving It* in 1995 and *Wrongfully Accused* in 1998). That same year, he landed his first television job, appearing in an episode of *Actor's Studio* called "Hannah." As with most actors of his generation, Leslie appeared in a number of live TV dramas, and in fact, was featured in 46 programs that year alone on such shows as *Suspense, Kraft Television Theatre, Lights Out* and *Robert Montgomery Presents.* These were called "the Golden Years of Television," but as Leslie recalled: "There was very little gold. We only got $75 or $100 per show."

His success on these programs inevitably led to Hollywood offers. In 1956, Paramount Pictures signed him to co-star as Thilbault with Kathryn Grayson in Michael Curtiz's *The Vagabond King*. Following his success in that role, he was signed to a long-term contract with MGM, who cast him opposite Glenn Ford in the suspense drama *Ransom!* (1956). Glenn, who would again act with Leslie in the western *The Sheepman* (1958), in which Leslie played the heavy, would later say of his fellow Canadian co-star: "Leslie was just great to work with. Leslie is a very versatile actor."

His other MGM credits included *The Opposite Sex* (1956) with Debbie Reynolds, and the lead role in the underrated crime thriller *Hot Summer Night* (1957). But Leslie's most famous role of the period was as Commander John J. Adams in the science-fiction classic *Forbidden Planet* (1956). Billed beneath Canadian-born Walter Pidgeon and the beauteous Anne Francis, Leslie gave a sterling performance as the leader of a space expedition sent from Earth to discover what happened to a colony of settlers on the planet Altair-4, only to discover two human survivors, Dr. Edward Morbius (Pidgeon) and his daughter Altaira (Francis). Interestingly, the movie's plot was derived from Shakespeare's *The Tempest*.

Forbidden Planet was an enormous success both critically and financially. But even the talents of Leslie and Walter Pidgeon and the visible assets of Anne Francis could not compete with the antics of Robbie the Robot, who became perhaps the most beloved science-fiction icon of the decade.

Leslie scored another commercial hit when he was loaned out to Universal-International to play pilot Peter Brent in *Tammy and the Bachelor* (1957), the love interest of Debbie Reynolds. Despite his growing success in movies, Leslie still kept busy with TV, continuing to advance in his craft while appearing in all the top shows of the day, including *Alfred Hitchcock Presents, Rawhide, Wagon Train, The Naked City* and *The Untouchables*. In his television ventures, Leslie was usually cast as the villain who received his comeuppance before the closing credits rolled. However, in 1959, he did a welcome about-face when he played the heroic General Francis Marion on Disney's highly rated miniseries *Swamp Fox*.

In 1958, Leslie married a third time, to Alisande Ullman, with whom he had two children. This marriage also ended in divorce, in 1973, as did his next union with Brooks Oliver, to whom he was married from 1981 to 1983. Leslie is currently very happily married to Joyce Collyer.

Leslie kept up a busy work schedule as he moved into the 1960s, concentrating on television and again turning in fine, serious performances on such programs as *Gunsmoke, Bonanza, Route 66, The F.B.I., Run for Your Life* and *Bob Hope Presents The Chrysler Theatre*. Again, he almost always played the bad guy with nary a trace of the comedy to come.

Beyond his guest roles, Leslie starred in seven series of his own, including *The New Breed* (1961–62), *Peyton Place* (1964–70), *The Protectors* (1969–70), *Bracken's World* (1970) and the miniseries *Backstairs at the White House* (1979) as Ike Hoover.

As to his film work, Leslie still remained on the dramatic track, most notably as the Howard Hughes–like character in *Harlow* (1965) and as Captain Harrison in the 1972 audience favourite *The Poseidon Adventure*.

Leslie also performed on the stage, starring with Carol Burnett in *Love Letters* (1990). Perhaps his most acclaimed stage role was as famed lawyer Clarence Darrow in the play *Darrow*. He took his one-man show on a national tour of the U.S. from September 1999 to February 2000. He also played two engagements in Europe, performing in Vienna, then a nine-week tour of England and Scotland that ran from March through May 2000. *Darrow* was artistically satisfying for Leslie. It was also one of his very few latter-day dramatic performances because, just years earlier, his career had taken an unexpected detour when he was offered a part in a movie that would revolutionize comedy.

Leslie Nielsen was quoted as saying: "Working with the Zuckers [brothers Jerry and David] and Jim Abrahams is the luckiest thing that ever happened to me. In the past, I'd watched reruns of the TV shows I'd done and couldn't help but laugh at the incredible gravity and seriousness—the characters all of a sudden became funny to me, including my own."

The opportunity Leslie was speaking about, of course, was his role in the enormously successful spoof of the *Airport* series—1980's *Airplane!* The Zucker-Abrahams-Zucker (or ZAZ) team hit upon a winning formula that scored with movie audiences and critics. In the 86-minute feature, the directors bombarded viewers with an endless parade of sight gags and ridiculous dialogue that poked fun at every disaster movie cliché. The jokes come so fast and furious that the movie must be watched several times to appreciate all of them. Leslie portrayed Dr. Rumack, and he fit right in with a supporting cast that included Robert Stack and Lloyd Bridges, both of whom had a ball spoofing their own images.

The humour in Leslie's performance was that he played it absolutely straight. His lines were delivered in a serious, sonorous intonation completely at odds with the ridiculous dialogue his character was speaking. Who can forget this simple yet memorable exchange between Leslie and Robert Hays' emotionally troubled pilot:

Hays: "Surely you can't be serious."
Leslie: "Yes I am. And don't call me Shirley."

With this one film, Leslie virtually disassociated himself from 30 years of dramatic roles in which his characters had rarely even cracked a smile.

Audiences embraced this new side of Leslie Nielsen that they'd never seen before, setting the actor off on a whole different career path—one that he'd secretly always wanted, but never thought he could possibly achieve.

Yet those who know Leslie personally maintain that he is one of the funniest people in the industry, with a bizarre sense of humour that is frequently displayed on television talk shows, most notably when he interrupts a serious conversation by suddenly releasing his omnipresent whoopee cushion.

He was a natural for zany comedy.

For his next screwball venture, Leslie returned to television to star as the inept Detective Frank Drebin in *Police Squad!* (1982). The series was every bit as much a farce as *Airplane!* (as well it should have been, since it was created by ZAZ). Unfortunately, the show didn't catch on with viewers and was cancelled after just one season. The failure of the series was bittersweet for Leslie, as he had been nominated for an Emmy for Outstanding Lead in a Comedy Series for *Police Squad!*

Leslie is one of those rare actors who can alternate successfully between film and television. He played health club owner Buddy Fox on the short-lived 1984 series *Shaping Up*. He was also seen as Katherine Helmond's boyfriend, Max Muldoon, on *Who's the Boss* and as Bea Arthur's romantic interest, Lucas Hollingsworth, whom she finally wed, on the final two episodes of *The Golden Girls* in the spring of 1992. In 1993, he even had the opportunity to play God on Fox's *Herman's Head* in the episode "God, Girls and Herman."

Perhaps his most personally satisfying television role came when he guested for two seasons (1995–96) on the CTV series *Due South*, in which he got to play Sergeant Buck Frobisher, a Mountie and a character he apparently patterned somewhat on his father.

Most recently, he appeared as host Terence Brynne McKennie on the Canadian Comedy Network's spoof of *Biography*, appropriately enough titled *Liography*. In the series, which had a brief run from 2001 to 2002, Leslie's character introduced fictional biographies that parodied celebrities' lives in the style made popular on the A&E program.

As goofy as Leslie plays it on television, he is completely over the top in his movie roles. Despite the premature cancellation of *Police Squad!*, ZAZ decided to bring the character of Frank Drebin to the big screen, and in 1988, they released *The Naked Gun: From the Files of Police Squad!* In the film, Leslie is surrounded by an intriguing cast that includes George Kennedy, Ricardo Montalban, Priscilla Presley and the infamous O.J. Simpson, who provides a surprisingly good comic turn. The film proved so popular that they released two sequels: *The Naked Gun 2$^1/_2$: The Smell of Fear* (1991) and *Naked Gun 33$^1/_3$: The Final Insult* (1994). Perhaps one of the reasons for the success of these films is that running at less than 90 minutes each, they don't wear out their welcome.

By now, Leslie's comic persona was firmly established. He continued playing zany parts in such films as the exorcism spoof *Repossessed* (1990), which co-starred original head-turner Linda Blair, the Mel Brooks–directed vampire lampoon *Dracula: Dead and Loving It* (1995), the spy takeoff *Spy Hard* (1996) and a parody of the Harrison Ford film *The Fugitive* called *Wrongfully Accused* (1998). He also appeared in weaker comedies such as *Soul Man* (1986) and *Surf Ninjas* (1993).

While Leslie has proven that comedy is his forte, he has turned in some fine dramatic appearances. Although his role was small, he was convincing as Jamie Lee Curtis' father in the 1980 Canadian-made stalker thriller *Prom Night.* He was also effective as the jealous husband whose scheme of revenge against his faithless wife and her lover backfires—with a vengeance—in the "Something To Tide You Over" episode of *Creepshow* (1982). Perhaps his most powerful dramatic role was as the sleazy john who is murdered by prostitute Barbra Streisand in Martin Ritt's *Nuts* (1987). On a lighter note, he played a pragmatic department store Santa Claus in the sentimental *All I Want for Christmas* (1991).

But despite these occasional forays into serious acting, Leslie continues to be recognized as a star of comedies. In 1995, he became the 18th recipient of UCLA's Jack Benny Award, joining such comedy greats as Johnny Carson, Steve Martin, George Burns and Carol Burnett.

Although Leslie has become a naturalized U.S. citizen, another honour of which he is most proud is his inclusion on Canada's Walk of Fame on June 1, 2001. Canada's appreciation of Leslie's success was further recognized when he received the Order of Canada in 2003. He even received honorary citizenship from Winnipeg mayor Glen Murray when he and fellow *Men with Brooms* co-star Paul Gross arrived in the city on a promotional tour for the film.

Leslie refuses to take his celebrity status seriously. This can best be proven within the pages of his 1993 "autobiography" *The Naked Truth*. In the book, Leslie tells hilarious stories about his life and career, only a few of which have a grain of truth.

Leslie, who has appeared in well over 100 TV and movie roles, has been honoured and revered by the motion picture industry and his millions of fans. It's clear that while he enjoys himself immensely acting in his silly comedies, his other motivation is to entertain his audience and provide them with an hour and a half of ridiculousness to help them forget their troubles.

And at this, Leslie Nielsen has succeeded beyond his wildest expectations.

It's a Wrap...

LESLIE NIELSEN AND THE OTHER ACTORS MENTIONED IN THIS book, along with other notables such as Marie Dressler, Walter Pidgeon, Ruby Keeler and Hume Cronyn have clearly displayed that there is a wealth of talent in Canada. While most moved on to expand both their opportunities and visibility in the U.S., talents such as Gordon Pinsent, singer Anne Murray and comedians Johnny Wayne and Frank Shuster have enjoyed solidly successful careers in their homeland.

Canada can feel proud of its entertainment heritage and those gifted performers who became "The Canadian Connection."

Notes on Sources

Books

Bennett, Linda Greene. *My Father's Voice: The Biography of Lorne Greene*. Lincoln, NE: iUniverse, 2004.

Hill, Ona L. *Raymond Burr: A Film, Radio and Television Biography*. Jefferson, NC: McFarland & Company, 1994.

Massey, Raymond. *When I Was Young*. Boston: Little, Brown & Company, 1976.

Nielsen, Leslie and David Fisher. *The Naked Truth*. NY: Pocket Books, 1993.

Pinsent, Gordon. *By the Way*. Toronto: Stoddart Publishing, 1992.

Quirk, Laurence J. *Norma: The Story of Norma Shearer*. New York: St. Martin's Press, 1988.

Whitfield, Eileen. *Pickford: The Woman Who Made Hollywood*. Lexington, KY: University Press of Kentucky, 1997.

Wray, Fay. *On The Other Hand*. London: Weidenfeld & Nicholson. 1989.

Websites

American Experience: Mary Pickford.
http://www.pbs.org/wgbh/amex/pickford/.

Answers.com. http://www.answers.com/.

Bonanza World. http://www.bonanzaworld.net/.

Christopher Plummer.com.
  http://www.christopherplummer.com/.

Glenn Ford: A Silver Screen Legend.
  http://www.glennfordonline.com/.

In Remembrance: Fay Wray.
  http://www.filmbuffonline.com/InRemembrance/
  FayWray.htm.

Internet Movie Database. http://www.imdb.com/.

Literary Encyclopedia. http://www.litencyc.com/.

CBC Life and Times of Gordon Pinsent.
  http://www.cbc.ca/lifeandtimes/pinsent.html.

Lorne Greene. http://bonanza1.com/lorne.html.

The Mary Pickford Foundation.
  http://www.marypickford.com/.

Museum of Broadcast Communications: Raymond
  Burr. http://www.museum.tv/archives/etv/B/htmlB/
  burrraymond/burrraymond.htm.

Northern Stars. http://northernstars.ca/.

Shearer Sophistication.
  http://www.geocities.com/Hollywood/Boulevard/
  5255/.

Talking Comedy with Leslie Nielsen.
  http://www.horschamp.qc.ca/new_offscreen/
  leslie.html

William Shatner.com. http://www.williamshatner.com/.